WHITE AND COLOURED

WHITE
AND COLOURED

The behavior of British people towards
coloured immigrants

by

MICHAEL BANTON

RUTGERS UNIVERSITY PRESS
NEW BRUNSWICK   NEW JERSEY
1960

CONTENTS

PREFACE   9

Part I: PERSONALITY AND SOCIETY

CHAPTER   I   Prejudice and Discrimination   15
       II   Explaining Prejudice   23
       III   Explaining Discrimination   39

Part II: THE UNSPOKEN LANGUAGE

CHAPTER   IV   Changing Conceptions of the Coloured Man   55
       V   The Archetypal Stranger   73
       VI   When Custom Fails   92

Part III: THE INTERRACIAL SCENE

CHAPTER   VII   Strangers in Dockland   117
       VIII   Race and Class at the Universities   138
       IX   Coloured Workers in Industrial Cities   157

Part IV: THE MEANING OF COLOUR

CHAPTER   X   Quod Erat Demonstrandum   177

Appendix I: Ten Commandments of Inter-Group Relations   187
Appendix II: British Racial Attitudes   197

NOTES AND REFERENCES   213
BIBLIOGRAPHY   217
INDEX   219

LIST OF TABLES

I Responses to statements intended to indicate the presence or absence of racial stereotypes   35

II The social distance of five stranger nationalities   89

III Sources of West Indian immigration, 1955-56   158

IV Coloured Commonwealth and Colonial population of Britain; estimates for *1st January*, 1959   159

V Responses to statements on immigration   203

VI Correlations between sex of respondents and friendliness towards immigrants   209

To
R. M. B

PREFACE

RELATIONS between white and coloured people in Britain abound in paradoxes:

Why should coloured people so often be shabbily treated when the vast majority of individual Britons are favourably disposed towards them?

Why should Britons be strongly opposed to any discrimination in the public treatment of coloured people and at the same time be so hesitant about treating them equally in private relations?

Why should British conduct towards coloured people be uncertain and inclined to change in so startling a fashion? For example, a hotel proprietor let rooms to three coloured students whose complexion was so light that they could not easily be recognized as coloured. After the arrangements had been completed he asked what country they came from. 'India,' they replied. Whereupon he turned them out and refused them their rooms. Sudden changes of front are not unusual. How are they to be accounted for?[1]

Why should individual Britons believe their fellows to be less favourably disposed towards coloured people than they themselves?

This book began as an attempt to review the available material on race relations in Britain — published and unpublished — and to ascertain what it taught us about British behaviour towards coloured immigrants. As the work progressed this aim gradually took second place to a consideration of certain theoretical issues which had to be cleared up before the original task could be completed. Several earlier writers had discussed the unfavourable treatment of coloured people as if it were the outcome of prejudice on the part of individual Britons. This interpretation seemed inadequate and indeed seriously misleading, so it became necessary to clarify the relation between psychological and

9

sociological explanations and define more explicitly the sociological problem presented by race relations. The way was then clear for an analysis of the significance that is attached to a dark skin colour in everyday social behaviour. What difference does it make to us if the person we have to deal with is a native-born white man, a European foreigner or a coloured man? The question cannot be answered by treating relations with coloured people as standing in a class by themselves; they have to be viewed in terms of a theory of the structure of British society, and should in their turn contribute something to the development of that theory.

Working along these lines, and taking into account changes in the relationship between Britons and coloured colonials, it has been possible to elaborate a series of propositions which help to explain the paradoxes set out above. These propositions, which turn on customary norms as to the rights and obligations of coloured men in particular relationships, are advanced in the second part of the book and have been stated in summary form in a final chapter. The available documentary material — reviewed in the third part — is not detailed enough to provide much more than a prima facie case in their support. They are advanced as hypotheses, and are none the worse for that, for in sociology as in any other science it is often harder to find the right question than the right answer.

Sometimes it is argued that the term 'race' should not be used in studies of social behaviour. Race, it is said, is a zoological category; a group of persons with a common national or regional background may not coincide with any racial group and so it is more properly termed an 'ethnic group'. Implicit in this recommendation is the view that biology and sociology are concerned with different phenomena, whereas it will here be maintained that they often deal with the same phenomena but from different standpoints. Race is not the only biological category to be used in social analyses; there are others — like those of age and sex — which are particularly relevant. But when he employs such terms the social scientist does not use them in exactly the same sense as the biologist; he is concerned with age or sex in so far as they are socially significant and not with all their physiological implications. So it is with race and colour. What 'race' means in biology may be left to the physical anthropologists and geneticists (some of whom doubt whether the concept is of any value at all). Whatever its significance in physiology, the possession of a coloured skin has definite connotations for the man in the street. And it is this, the meaning of colour in contemporary British social life, that the present study seeks to elucidate.

The work was undertaken at the suggestion of Dr Kenneth Little, Head of the Department of Social Anthropology in the University of Edinburgh, and was assisted by a grant from the Nuffield Foundation which made it possible to carry out the racial attitudes survey. Mrs Mary Klopper worked as a part-time research assistant during 1956–57 and was of the greatest help in looking after the administrative side of the survey and computing the results. To Dr Little I am obliged for permission to use and quote from the reports of Miss Sheila Webster (now Mrs U. Kitzinger), Miss Violaine Junod and Mr E. B. Ndem, respecting investigations undertaken for the Department of Social Anthropology between 1951 and 1953. But I am much more indebted to Dr Little for his kindly encouragement and tolerance over the past eight years, and for his friendly criticism at various stages in the development of this inquiry.

Dr Cecil Gordon and Mr George Shepperson kindly commented on Chapter IV in draft. My thanks are further due to the fifty people who constituted the judges' panel for the assessment of responses in the attitudes survey.

I should also like to take this opportunity of acknowledging my indebtedness to my teachers at the London School of Economics, especially Professors Raymond Firth, Morris Ginsberg and K. R. Popper; to Dr Edward A. Shils for introducing me to the study of sociology, and Mr D. G. MacRae and Professor D. V. Glass for encouraging me to pursue it. How much I owe to my colleagues at the Social Sciences Research Centre, University of Edinburgh, I cannot tell, except that it is considerably more than I had any right to expect. Mention of any particular names in such a context is invidious, but I cannot pass over the help I have derived from discussions with Mr R.

M. McKenzie of the relation between psychology and sociology, and from his advice and assistance in analysing the results of the survey; for its deficiencies he is in no way responsible. Nor can I ignore my debt to Mr Tom Burns's pioneer work on the sociological study of face-to-face relations.

M. P. B.

Social Sciences Research Centre,
University of Edinburgh.

December, 1958.

Part I

PERSONALITY AND SOCIETY

CHAPTER I

PREJUDICE AND DISCRIMINATION

Prejudice, like race, has only marginal relevance to race relations. Race relations are not based on prejudice; prejudice is a by-product of race relations — as influenced by other factors.   CAREY MCWILLIAMS[1]

THE study of race relations may be regarded as one of the applied social sciences. It has no specific theoretical lines of inquiry, as psychology, sociology and economics have, but seeks to apply the theories developed in these schools to the elucidation of particular problems. The student of psychology, however, may see in situations of racial contact an excellent field for testing out some of his theories about personality structure; his main interest is not in race relations but in psychology, and he may be pardoned if he sees everything from a psychological point of view. The same may be said of the economist — or, rather, of certain varieties of economist. Indeed, the scientific study of race relations in recent decades has been dominated by writers with either a psychological or an economic orientation.

This debate has sometimes been presented as if it were a question of choosing between an economic and a psychological interpretation of racial conflict. The two approaches have been seen as competing with each other in offering the correct explanation. This is a serious misconception. Advocates of the two approaches have in fact not been concerned with the same problem, but have dealt with different aspects of it. One consequence of the failure to appreciate that the social scientist's interest is restricted to just an aspect of an event, or series of events, has been the neglect of other relevant aspects. The sociology of race relations has suffered considerably from the idea that all could be explained in terms of economics or of psychology. Many of the sociological textbooks in this field present chiefly descriptive material of a kind that could be collected by any educated person; they do not give evidence of any specific sociological skills which contribute an understanding that could be obtained through no other discipline. One aim of the present work is to show that there is a specifically sociological contribution and to attempt to define it more closely than has been done hitherto. We shall show that sociological factors are of particular importance to an analysis of race relations in contemporary Britain, but, because this is the focus of our interest, we shall not consider non-sociological factors in equal detail.

In writing of psychology, sociology and economics as separate subjects we do not seek to revive a barren controversy about the nature and boundaries of particular social sciences. In an important sense only the problems are real, and the organization of teaching and research in different sets of problems is just a matter of convention. Nevertheless, psychologists, sociologists and economists do concentrate upon different aspects of social behaviour and it is helpful to try and pinpoint the standpoints they usually adopt. Of course, it frequently happens that problems intermediate between two traditional fields of inquiry assume a novel importance and a new science grows up, but before this can happen some new and significant aspect has to be identified.

In studying racial antagonism, psychologists and sociologists both start from observed behaviour. Psychologists have usually concentrated upon the motivations of the people involved; often they have inferred that they were actuated by prejudice. Sociologists are interested in the differential treatment of persons ascribed to particular categories, which is conceptualized as discrimination. Discrimination interests the sociologist only in so far as it constitutes a social pattern; the idiosyncrasy of a few isolated individuals in discriminating against, say, redheads, would not be of interest. Prejudice and discrimination are often found together, for each encourages the other, but they are theoretically quite separate aspects of behaviour. Prejudiced people do not necessarily discriminate. Someone accustomed to treating coloured people in an inferior fashion will mend his ways in a country where he knows that such behaviour will be disapproved, or punished. The release of hostility is regulated by social factors, so that people give vent to their feelings only in those situations that are thought to be appropriate. But discrimination is not necessarily the outcome of prejudice. It may be that an actor is forced to behave contrary to his own preferences, or that he has reasons for his action which have nothing to do with his own attitudes towards the group in question. Discrimination is a feature of certain kinds of behaviour objectively considered, and is independent of questions of intention or moral justification.[2]

A couple of examples will make thus usage clearer. A hotel manager may refuse accommodation to coloured people, but we cannot infer from this that he is prejudiced. He may only be carrying out the proprietor's instructions. The proprietor may himself be well-disposed towards coloured people but have them turned away because he is afraid of losing white custom. We can never with certainty infer the actor's intention from observing his behaviour. 'Prejudice' refers to a state of mind, a disposition unfavourable to certain persons, which may or may not find outlet in hostile behaviour. However, we can say that, whatever the intention or the disposition of the man responsible, any act that excludes coloured people from a hotel because they are coloured is discriminatory. This does not mean that it is necessarily wrongful. An employer engaging new workmen might believe that if he took too many coloured men his existing workers would make trouble. Rather than risk exciting racial antagonism he might restrict the number of coloured workers to a certain proportion of the labour strength; when this limit had been reached he would turn away coloured job seekers although they were individually as well qualified as white workmen whom he accepted. In doing so he would be discriminating against them; the possibility that in the long run the minority might benefit from such a policy may be relevant to a moral judgment, but it does not alter the discriminatory character of the action. Many similar situations can be conceived. Whether or not they are of frequent occurrence is not now at issue, but their feasibility is sufficient to demonstrate the independence of prejudice and discrimination.

Many psychological writers have thought of individual disposition as the dynamic element in behaviour ultimately responsible for inter-group antagonism, and have seen social factors as repressing, permitting or encouraging the display of this disposition. We may draw an analogy with water flowing along a pipe; for the psychologist, individual disposition constitutes the flow while social factors are a tap which may turn it down or boost it up. Sociologists see things the other way about. They have tended to argue, for example, that a white man in the American South will act aggressively towards a Negro who claims privileges customarily reserved to whites. To explain apparently contrary instances they may introduce qualifications about the role of non-sociological factors, such as: 'provided these persons do not have economic interests which are thereby seriously endangered'; or, 'provided that they have no strong emotional predisposition in favour of Negroes'. In this case it is the structure of the situation which is singled out and seen as the flow along the pipe; individual and other factors are regarded as resembling the tap which modifies the flow. This isolation of one factor at a time is the only way to carry out a scientific investigation, for nothing can be examined from two standpoints simultaneously.

From these premises it follows that the problem of how to explain cases of prejudice is quite separate from that of explaining discrimination. The former is conventionally the task of the psychologist, the latter of the sociologist. The two examine the same data, the same 'facts', but from different aspects, each singling out the variable that interests him and viewing other influences only as modifying factors. The point which we wish to emphasize — for it is often overlooked — is that this is a characteristic of the method of investigation, not a characteristic of things as they exist in the world. The psychologist thinks of social factors as the 'tap' regulating the expression of individual dispositions, but this does not mean that the task of sociology is no more than to explain why in given situations the tap is open or closed, or why the flow of hostility is directed upon one group rather than another. The sociological approach lies in a different way of looking at the same phenomena and in isolating a different variable.

How is the sociological approach defined? Sometimes it is said that psychology deals with individuals, sociology with groups or with societies. That way lies confusion. The existence of a group is an inference from observation and it is usually difficult to fix its boundaries.

The term 'individual', however, is used to refer to both a real thing and an abstraction, and the failure to distinguish between these usages has given rise to several false problems. For the unique human being, the real thing, we prefer to use the term 'actor' and reserve 'individual' for the psychologist's concept of the actor considered as if he existed in isolation from society. This usage may seem awkward at first but we believe that the distinction between the actor and the individual (and that between the actor and the person to be outlined shortly) will help the reader to appreciate that the social sciences — psychology included — each study certain general features of human activities; they disregard the uniqueness of particular human beings although it is they, and not the abstractions, who make up real situations. We can formulate a more satisfactory view of the relations between the social sciences by saying that they all take social behaviour as their subject matter but view it from different aspects, isolating different variables. Any social action whatsoever can be studied from the viewpoint of any of the social sciences, though in the vast majority of cases only certain aspects will be of any scientific or practical significance.

Let us take a simple example involving only one actor: a man sets a plate of food before his dog. The geographer might see this as exemplifying a regional custom — only in certain parts of the world do people keep dogs as pets and feed them. That the action occurred in a particular place may be explained by referring it to regional patterns of this kind. The economist might consider the action as an allocation of scarce resources, explaining the quantity of meat provided or the amount of meat relative to potatoes. The psychologist might concentrate upon the actor's desire for company, or the satisfaction he got from looking after a dependent creature, and the action might be explained as a response to such feelings. The sociologist might see in it evidence of the duties of a dog-owner, enforced by such sanctions as public opinion and the R.S.P.C.A. can command. These various explanations are not in conflict. Different students see in the same action different problems, though they frequently fail to make explicit the aspects upon which they are concentrating.

The geographer is interested in the actor in so far as his behaviour can be related to factors of place. The economist studies the consequences of the actor's allocating his scarce resources in a given manner. The psychologist examines the actor as an individual, relating his behaviour to his physical or mental make-up, in which the effects of past experience may play an important part. The sociologist concentrates upon the actor as a person, in a sense similar to the legal use of the term. Jurists mean by a 'person' (to follow the *Oxford Dictionary*) a 'human being with recognized rights and duties'. Any actor will be many social persons in the sense of having various sets of rights and duties ('Unus homo plures personas sustinet' — as the lawyers say). In a legal situation only one such set will normally be put in question — say, an actor's rights and duties as an employer (but not as a married man), or as a husband (but not as an employer).

In this we follow S. F. Nadel, who shows that, so considered, the person is more than the actor; it is the actor with certain recognized, or institutionalized, tasks and relationships, and it is *all* the actors who behave in that way. The person is also less than the actor; for an actor may be several persons, and out of his physical and mental qualities only some will enter into the ways of acting which define the person. The 'landlord', or 'tenant', or 'debtor', or 'husband', or 'father', are persons, who at any given moment are represented in numerous actors; yet the same man may be tenant, debtor, husband, father, all at once and with different parts of his being, acting as one or the other in different contexts and in respect of different other persons.[3] Nadel saw clearly what must be the main application of this insight in the sociological field. A society, as he points out, can be conceptualized as a structure of persons. When sociologists single out the structure of the situation as a factor exerting causal influence upon behaviour, they see it as defined by people's expectations of particular modes of conduct and the sanctions that can be directed against actors who fail to behave in the prescribed manner. Certain rights and obligations are enforceable at law, but there are many more which depend upon convention and are supported by informal sanctions. Sociologists have a particular interest in the implicit social norms that express customary obligations;

thus they share certain common interests with students of jurisprudence.

Discrimination, as we said, is the differential treatment of particular persons. In Alabama the Negro and the white man are different persons, for they have different rights and duties. In Britain the idea of discrimination against red-heads seems unreal because it is difficult to conceive of them as ever being distinctive persons in the sociological sense. Discrimination against West Indians, however, becomes feasible whenever they are thought of as constituting a separate social category, which is the same as saying that people think that they have different obligations towards them than towards Britons (however slight the difference) or that the West Indians have different obligations towards Britons than do other residents in the country. It is along these lines that the sociologist has his distinctive contribution to make to the analysis of relations between different racial groups.

One further consequence of our premises remains to be made explicit. Science is selective in its interests, and the social sciences deal only with aspects of behaviour. We have suggested that a variety of different aspects of a man's action in feeding his dog could be explained, but even if every conceivable aspect were studied and the various explanations gathered together it would not be possible to say that the whole action had been explained, for the number of aspects that any action presents is in principle infinite. Moreover, we should still be unable to say *why* the man fed his dog, because while science can explain motivation it can never explain intention.[4] To emphasize the limitations of science is important because some writers have thought that their theories explained more than they really did. It also reveals the importance of the extra-scientific. The legislator, the administrator and the citizen are presented with problems as wholes; they need some understanding of the whole if they are to decide which aspects are most important and which scientists can contribute most towards a solution. This synoptic view of the whole cannot be scientific but must be philosophical in character — whether the philosophy be explicit or not. This deserves reiteration because, influenced by the nineteenth-century encyclopedists Auguste Comte and Herbert Spencer, many people still believe that sociology's task is the synthesis of all the sciences, or that its fundamental concern is with elaborating a new morality. Our argument, however, is in line with an older sociological tradition which goes back to Montesquieu and has been revived in our own day by British social anthropologists, most notably by A. R. Radcliffe-Brown.

CHAPTER II

EXPLAINING PREJUDICE

The Negro is the white man's fear of himself.   O. MANNONI[1]

THE word 'prejudice' is derived from the Latin 'praejudiciums' which meant a precedent, a judgment based on previous decision, and experiences. In English the word came to mean a prejudgment and it is still sometimes understood in this sense, though it will be clear upon reflection that this is not its normal meaning, for prejudgments are necessary in almost everything we do, whereas no one could claim the same for prejudices. Prejudgments become prejudices only if they are not subject to modification in the light of new experience. One of the major characteristics of prejudice is this mental rigidity which the prejudiced individual maintains by twisting new information to accord with his stereotyped preconceptions.

Many different theories of racial prejudice have been advanced, but they fall into two principal categories. This classification we owe to John Dollard,[2] one of the founders of the scientific study of the subject. He wrote: 'Close analysis of the word [race prejudice] reveals at least two distinct situations in which it is used: one where irrational antagonism is vented against other people, and the other where rational, that is intelligible, hostility is aroused in defence of a given status or economic order.' The latter situation gave rise to a form of behaviour he termed *direct aggression*, as opposed to the former which was one of *displaced aggression*. In situations of direct aggression the individual identified his opponent and attacked him. The competition in towns of the American South for 'white man's jobs' was a case in point, for, according to Dollard, real animosity was manifested against the competing Negro workers and political measures were adopted to limit their ability to compete. In situations of displaced aggression, on the other hand, the individual did not attack the frustrating agent but displaced his resentment on to a scapegoat. This might be because the frustrating agent was too powerful, or because the frustration came from within the individual's own social group and he valued his membership too much to risk losing it. The assumption of displacement then enabled the psychologist to interpret situations where groups show animosity without having any direct reason for doing so. According to writers of the Freudian persuasion all members of societies have to repress some of their individualistic impulses and to accept a degree of frustration which cannot be vented upon the frustrating agent. Hence there is always a fund of potential hostility, and so wherever direct aggression is released there will be a certain amount of displaced aggression accompanying it and adding extra force to the rational attack.

In its simplest form the frustration–aggression theory holds that when an individual's attempts to achieve satisfaction are interfered with this generates aggression; if it cannot be released in an attack upon the individual or group responsible for the interference it is displaced on to a scapegoat. Why one particular group rather than another should be chosen is explained in terms of its visibility, its vulnerability, and its tendency to symbolize the true source of frustration. To this it has been objected that the terms are apt to be used too loosely: if anyone behaves aggressively it is all too easy to postulate frustration as the cause, and when experimental tests have been set up it has not proved easy to define aggression. Moreover, frustration leads to responses other than aggression and does not always produce aggression. Jews, for example, are as a group subject to special frustrations, but instead of showing the more hostility to other minorities, they tend to identify themselves with them. Nor does displacement of aggression actually relieve the feeling of frustration as the theory seems to suggest. Of particular importance, too, is the fact that it has proved impossible to demonstrate that those individuals who have marked prejudices have endured greater frustrations than others. However, the utility of the frustration–displaced aggression hypothesis is restricted most severely by its invalidity in some social situations. Much depends upon whether the culture of a group permits the discharge of hostility on to a scapegoat. In parts of Brazil, where there is a high general level of tolerance, there are whites who in economic terms are much more frustrated than in the United States, but they do not attempt to compensate for it by attacking the Negroes or other minorities. Where social distance and hostility between racial groups is institutionalized, as in the southern districts of the United States, it may be the 'poor whites' who display most aggression, but this must be seen in relation to a social setting and power structure which condone and even support or encourage the attacks. In general, well-to-do people, who could not be considered 'frustrated' by the same criteria used to define the 'poor white' category, have rarely shown any opposition to lynching and have not infrequently instigated it. Nevertheless, in the study of any single situation it seems probable that the degree of *manifestation* of prejudice may be related, among other factors, to the incidence of frustration.

At the close of the paper in which Dollard distinguished between the two situations with which prejudice is associated, he said, referring to his earlier classic work *Caste and Class in a Southern Town*: 'I was able to see only the irrational or displaced aggressive components of the reaction. Criticism from other students has compelled me to see the role of actual rivalry in prejudice situations and to attempt to do it more justice.' Later writers, however, have ignored Dollard's second thoughts, dealing in detail with displacement but neglecting the question of direct aggression. Fifty years ago the irrational components of behaviour were seriously underestimated; since then Freud has taught us how important irrational factors can be, and now some social scientists never look beyond them.

As an example of how far some psychologists at one time went in emphasizing the irrational features of prejudice as a personality characteristic we may cite the extraordinary observation of Gardner Murphy that ' ... there is really no such thing as Negro prejudice or anti-Semitism – except as an expression of purely negative reality, like a vitamin deficiency. There is an acute absence of something, namely of the normal human interchange of ideas or feelings; there is a system of barriers. These barriers, however, are usually of the same general type and arise in about the same way regardless of the type of religious or racial hostility involved.' The passage illustrates well the dangers of confusing a characterization of one aspect of prejudice with an account

25

of prejudice as a totality. It is taken from the preface to a book by E. L. Hartley,[3] published in New York in 1946, which gives the results of an experiment involving over six hundred students. They had completed a modified version of the Bogardus Social Distance Test, in which subjects are required to indicate how close a degree of contact with various groups they would be willing to accept. There is a scale beginning 'I would admit a member of this group: 1. to close kinship by marriage; 2. to my club as personal chums; 3. to my street as neighbours ... etc.' It has been found that most Americans find Englishmen and Canadians acceptable as social equals and kinsmen, whereas Hindus, Turks and Negroes fall at the other end of the scale. Hartley ascertained the students' attitudes towards thirty-two nations and racial groups but added to the list three fictitious names 'Danireans', 'Pireneans' and 'Wallonians'. It turned out that the students who wished to keep the familiar ethnic groups at a distance were also inclined to reject the imaginary peoples. Another part of the experiment indicated that these students also tended to have particular personality characteristics.

Hartley's experiment has been cited as proving that 'prejudice is a generalized attitude having its basis in the individual who expresses it rather than in the groups to whom the prejudice is directed'. This is not a legitimate inference. Attitudes towards the stranger groups were assessed in the context of a test which presented them as immigrants seeking admission to the United States. It encouraged the subject to view the degree of acceptance as something he could decide impersonally, which is very different from his having to deal with a real individual who has laid claim to being treated in a particular way. In the test situation the expression of distance with regard to any of the groups listed was socially permissible. Nevertheless there were appreciable variations in the level of tolerance of students at different colleges. The author himself was aware of the danger of generalizing from his material, for he remarks that 'students at one school, ranking Jews towards the bottom of their schedule of preferences, were objectively responding towards this religious minority more favourably than the students of another school were responding towards Danes, though in the latter school Danes ranked towards the top of the list of preferences'. Prejudice may be a generalized attitude in individuals, but it is also a relationship. People cannot conceive of Danireans and Wallonians existing in the abstract, but only in some particular relationship to themselves. Prejudice can arise only in a social context and must be related to that context; it can never be inferred from the results of social distance tests because these measure a disposition to discriminate.

Writers inclined towards psychoanalytic interpretations of behaviour have suggested that strongly prejudiced individuals are in the main those who have suffered from a bad home background during childhood years, their parents having been on bad terms with one another, the child rejected by one or the other of them and deprived of affection. The prejudice they develop later in life represents an attempt to 'restore a crippled self', something used as a defence mechanism in an attempt to allay their own anxieties. At the same time prejudiced individuals try to gain strength by associating or identifying themselves with groups that are seen as powerful and dominant. Thus they are often people who conform strictly to social convention.

This question of why some people develop prejudice rather than others has been illuminated by the results of an intensive inquiry showing how certain personality characteristics tend to be associated with the expression of anti-Semitic opinions. The authors of *The Authoritarian Personality*[4] found that individuals' tendencies to anti-Semitism could be measured fairly accurately by a scale constructed to yield an estimate of receptivity to fascist ideology. Nine features of the characteristic fascist personality are listed:

Conventionalism: rigid adherence to conventional middle-class values.

Authoritarian submission: submissive, uncritical attitude towards idealized moral authorities of the in-group.

Authoritarian aggression: tendency to be on the look-out for, and to condemn, reject and punish people who violate conventional values.

Anti-intraception: opposition to the subjective, the imaginative, the tender-minded.

Superstition and stereotypy: the belief in mystical determinants of the individual's fate; the disposition to think in rigid categories.

Power and 'toughness': preoccupation with the dominance–submission, strong–weak, leader–follower dimension; identification with power figures; overemphasis upon the conventionalized attributes of the ego; exaggerated assertion of strength and toughness.

Destructiveness and cynicism: generalized hostility; vilification of the human.

Projectivity: the disposition to believe that wild and dangerous things go on in the world; the projection outwards of unconscious emotional impulses.

Sex: exaggerated concern with sexual 'goings on'.

Professor H. J. Eysenck[5] has held that on some issues the authoritarian anti-fascist holds very similar opinions to the fascist and that there are in fact two dimensions on which attitudes are to be measured: Radical–Conservative, and Tough-minded–Tender-minded. On the first axis we find that adherence to the radical view in politics is associated with less strict views about sexual morality. Towards the Tender-minded end of the second axis we note that people who consider the death penalty barbaric are also apt to favour compulsory religious instruction. Those who hold that coloured people are inferior and who are inclined to prejudice are better classified as Conservative-Tough-minded than as fascist, as this brings out both dimensions. The data and deductions on which these conclusions are based have, however, been subject to severe criticism.[6]

It will be noticed that Eysenck's theory belongs to the realm of pure psychology; it depends upon no economic or sociological assumptions but states necessary relations between sets of attitudes. An extension of it to comprehend personality variations in other cultures might result in its modification, but it would remain a theory of personality considered in isolation. To apply it to the explanation of particular problems, non-psychological assumptions would have to be introduced.

A notable attempt to formulate a theory of prejudice which gives explicit consideration to the role of non-psychological factors was made by Dr James H. Robb[7] in his study of anti-Semitism in a working-class London borough. He concluded that: (i) a predisposition to open hostility towards out-groups is formed when early childhood and late social experiences do not produce sufficient affection and security to meet the needs of the personality; (ii) this hostility will be directed towards Jewish groups (a) when such groups are observable within the individual's social field, and (b) when such hostility does not result in punishment by people whose support is important to the man showing hostility — otherwise another target may be chosen; (iii) the characteristics attributed to the Jewish group under these circumstances are likely to reflect some of the needs and repressed wishes of the hostile individual. Dr Robb at the same time drew attention to the importance of social factors. Situations which are felt as deprivation, he pointed out, are likely to vary from country to country, class to class, and also, within the same milieu, from one time to another. Historical and social movements influence anti-Semitism by affecting predisposed persons, but the precipitating factor may be an unrelated incident such as a deserting wife, an ungrateful child or dismissal from a friendship group.

A characteristic of these and similar psychological theories is that they have been elaborated with reference to situations where there is some general agreement about the status of the group on to whom aggression is displaced, and relations between the two groups have to some extent been institutionalized so that any relationship between a member of one and a member of the other has a certain significance given to it by custom. It would be interesting to have comparable investigations carried out in regions where inter-group relations have not become conventionalized to the same extent.

In recent years the word 'prejudice' has acquired a decidedly emotional significance, as denoting an attitude of mind that is unfair to others. A man who discriminates against a minority group is most reluctant to admit to prejudice and will try to explain his behaviour by reference to objective factors only. Prejudice has become something of a bogy word. This, of course, is nothing new in sociology, for, as has been said, our concepts often tend to become epithets. But it has led some writers to abandon the use of the word altogether. One influential school discards the term and speaks of such individuals as ethnocentric. The authors of one American book say that now, thanks to the human relations experts, the word prejudice has acquired such an aura of ceremonial that they prefer to substitute the word 'hate'. Elsewhere an attempt has been made to define prejudice as a set of attitudes leading to the mistreatment of other peoples; this obscures the distinction between motivation and behaviour. To drop the word prejudice because of the associations it has acquired and substitute another would in the long run only lead to the devaluation of the new term.

It may be argued with more justification that the term prejudice has in recent sociopsychological research acquired a meaning that is both distinct and constructive. As Robb says: 'All the theories and all the evidence provided by research suggest that in anti-Semitism the irrational elements are the most important, that prejudice is not a negative thing, an absence of knowledge, but rather something positive, the fulfilment of a need.' If we know enough about an individual's make-up we can say whether or not he is likely to be inclined to prejudice in a given social situation. The cause is in the subject, not in the object of prejudice. It is an irrational, pathological phenomenon, arising from the individual's own inadequacies and resulting in displaced aggression. But if we use the word in this way we need another one to denote milder manifestations of hostility. We have suggested that this is found in the word 'antipathy', used in a sense opposite to that of 'sympathy'. Antipathy may be motivated by ignorance, by economic interests, by a desire to maintain group exclusiveness or prestige, and so on. As an attitude it is arrived at in a rational way, and the cause lies in the object of aggression or in the subject's image of the object; attitudes of this kind are culturally and socially transmitted, whereas prejudice, as Robb shows, is not. Antipathy results in direct aggression and can be modified by rational processes, such as education, whereas prejudice cannot be dispelled without treating the individual's psychic imbalance. The distinction between antipathy and prejudice is important even if only for its significance in the reduction of racial tensions, for a measure that might result in greater harmony in a situation characterized by antipathy might have quite other effects in one of prejudice. In the former situation people's objective discontents can be relieved, or their ignorance removed; but where, as in the latter case, feelings of hostility are strongly rooted in the unconscious an educational programme designed to show the scapegoat group in a more favourable light might result either in an increase of hostility or its transference on to another minority.

Prejudice may thus be defined as an emotional and rigidly hostile disposition towards members of a given group. It is not a value judgment in the sense that a liberal may be said to be prejudiced in favour of tolerance. Antipathy is a predisposition unfavourable to a particular group resulting from ignorance, conflict of interests or some other objective cause, and can be modified by favourable experience of members of the group in question.

The results of Robb's inquiry indicate that the same personality features as characterize the extreme anti-Semites were also found, though to a lesser degree, amongst the relatively less hostile. He scouts any suggestion that prejudice may be the result of ignorance, but leaves room in his theory for 'people whose prejudice is based on misinformation'. The ignorance or misinformation which may underlie antipathy is not a lack of information in the sense that information is provided by a schoolmaster to his class; rather is it a lack of the personal experience and understanding gained by contact with the strangers in everyday relations. Neither 'prejudice' nor 'antipathy' has any meaning unless the group against which it is directed is specified. Both terms apply to relations between social groups and not to relations between individuals: prejudice is directed against a person because he is a member of a particular group, not because of his individual characteristics, though these may also be the object of dislike. Dr Robb utilizes a psychological model for the study of anti-Semitism, isolating personality factors as being of the greatest interest to himself and taking account of others only in so far as they qualify the operation of these factors. This approach is legitimate and proper for a psychologist. The sociologist has cause for complaint only when it is claimed that a complete explanation can be found in factors of personality.

An approach to the study of British attitudes and behaviour towards coloured people which builds upon the research discussed above has been elaborated by Mr Anthony H. Richmond in his *Colour Prejudice in Britain*. He takes as his starting point the fact that some individuals express strongly antipathetic attitudes towards Negroes or other 'out-groups'. This is due to three principal factors: (i) where two or more groups are in contact people tend to identify themselves with their 'own' group; (ii) the individual's feelings of security derive from the degree of his acceptance by his own group, the anxiety resulting from insecurity may cause him to show hostility towards people who are not members of his own group;[8] (iii) the experiences of group life lead an individual to see members of out-groups in terms of his own group's stereotype of them. Mr Richmond then shows that in Britain antagonism towards coloured people is more marked in some spheres than in others. Prejudicial attitudes are encouraged by circumstances which threaten an individual's sense of security. The fear of unemployment makes white workers resent the Negro's presence, while groups that consider they have suffered from the immigrants' competition are the most likely to show hostility. He continues: 'it is the fact that the coloured workers are associated in the minds of others with menial tasks and inferior status, as well as with competition, which provides the real threat to the white worker's sense of security'. The same applies to prejudice against Negroes as neighbours and sex partners. Association with them is viewed with disfavour and 'the need among white people (especially those who are already insecure in their own lives) for the approval of others of their own class and ethnic group is so great that they dare not do anything which might result in disapproval'. Similarly, interpersonal relations of a sexual character provide an important source of security, but the stability of the existing pattern of relations is upset by the appearance of a rival group.

This theory, like Dr Robb's, employs a psychological model, being chiefly concerned with the way personal insecurity underlies the expression of prejudicial attitudes. The role of social factors as creating insecurity is explicitly recognized; the existence of the fear of unemployment, the fact that coloured workers are associated with menial tasks, etc., is taken as given. This, again, is necessary if the variable of chief interest is to be isolated. Mr Richmond has to make a separate approach to the questions of why the fear of unemployment should be so persistent on Merseyside, why coloured workers should be associated with menial tasks, and why coloured workers should appear a particular threat to patterns of sexual behaviour — any more than, say, the Irish immigrants who are numerous in the region.

Mr Richmond appreciates that this approach is limited to the explanation of prejudicial attitudes. Discriminatory behaviour may, as he points out, stem from quite different sources. Whereas factors connected with social or sexual security seem to be ultimately responsible for prejudice, the predominating factor governing acts of discrimination is in most cases economic. When there is a shortage of labour the employer no longer worries so much about the colour of an employee's skin. When his premises are banned to white troops the dance-hall manager who had previously admitted coloured servicemen decides to change his policy. It is unfortunate that this distinction is not developed further, for, if any 'act of deprivation directed towards Negroes individually' be regarded as discriminatory, then a landlady's turning away a would-be lodger, or a girl's declining a coloured man's invitation to dance, is also an act of discrimination and may not be motivated by prejudice. Had Mr Richmond pursued this question he might have arrived at a position similar to that advanced here. As it is, his approach and the presentation of his argument tends to suggest that far more can be accounted for in terms of prejudicial attitudes than we believe to be the case.[9]

As an illustration of the dangers of overemphasizing the role of attitudes we may consider in greater detail the question of group stereotypes. The word 'stereotype' can be used in two senses:[10] (a) to refer to a tendency for a given belief to be widespread in a society; (b) to refer to a tendency for a belief to be oversimplified in content and unresponsive to the objective factors. It is in this second sense that Mr Richmond used the word, for he refers to stereotypes as 'rigid

C   33

concepts governing the thought and behaviour of people towards others', and writes: 'stereotyped attitudes towards others are not modified by the mere acquisition of knowledge which contradicts the stereotype'. But it is doubtful whether, as Mr Richmond holds, stereotypes in this second, rigid sense, arise from the subject's group membership. He will perceive members of out-groups in a way that is influenced by the structure of social relationships, but personality factors are often decisive. Prejudiced individuals may live next door to tolerant people and be involved in the similar social relationships, and yet they are unwilling or unable to modify their rigid perceptions of out-group members.

Without stereotypes in this second sense there can be no prejudice, for prejudice is differentiated from mere prejudgment by the rigidity with which the individual maintains his preconceived interpretations. It is in this connection that the concept of stereotype has been most illuminating, and to use the same word in the weaker sense of denoting a widespread belief is only to debase a serviceable if troublesome piece of psychological currency. While relying heavily upon the concept, Mr Richmond often fails to make clear in which sense it is being used. In *The Colour Problem* we are told that 'many people in Britain' subscribe to six 'false stereotypes', as follows: coloured colonials are pagan; coloured colonials are uncivilized; coloured colonials have strong sexual urges; coloured colonials are ignorant; the colonies are economically weak and dependent; the colonies are full of wild animals. Five of these are the product of a faulty educational system, but 'stereotypes about Negro sexuality come into a different category altogether; they are ... an expression of deep-seated emotional conflicts concerning sexual matters'.

As the prevalence of stereotypes is a crucial consideration for any attempt to decide how important are the psychological factors in inter-group antagonism, we attempted to obtain some data on this in the course of an attitude survey which is described in greater detail later on. Subjects representative of the general British population were presented with three cards, each bearing ten statements about immigration, coloured people and relations between the two groups; they were

34

asked to indicate those statements which represented their own views. The rates of response to the statements bearing most closely upon the question of stereotypes are set out in the adjoining table.

Not all of Mr Richmond's six postulated stereotypes were included and the wording was occasionally altered to make it easier for the person interviewed to assent to either the positive or the negative version of the statement. The test was very crude and might have been planned more carefully, but taken in consideration with the comments made by subjects the result is quite unambiguous. That 'the coloured people who come here are uncivilized' was accepted by only eleven

TABLE I

Responses to Statements Intended to Indicate the Presence or Absence of Racial Stereotypes

Response Rate per cent	Statement
76	Coloured people are just as good as us when they have the same training and opportunities.
68	A lot of the coloured people here are very clever.
52	Coloured peoples from different countries are quite different from each other.
30	Coloured people have stronger sexual urges than white people.
16	All the coloured people in Britain are pretty much the same.
10	Coloured people will always be inferior to white people.
9	Most of the coloured people here are very ignorant.
9	Coloured people do not have stronger sexual urges than white people.
4	The coloured people who come here are uncivilized.

people out of three hundred — 3·7 per cent — and several of them apparently assented to it only through a misunderstanding. The view that coloured colonials are ignorant also received remarkably little support; the contrary proposition received a very great deal. It is improbable that stereotyped thinking is widespread when so many people regard coloured peoples from different countries as quite different from each other, and reject the contrary proposition, and when the most popular statement of all is that expressing the equality of white and coloured people. The postulated stereotype that 'most people in Britain believe that coloured colonials are pagans' was not adequately tested. It was discovered during a pilot survey that many people did not know the meaning of the word pagan, so the statement was amended to read 'the Africans and West Indians have their own religions at home', but as many people interpreted this to include Christianity it did not prove satisfactory: 36 per cent assented to this statement and 24 per cent to a contrary one stating that they were 'nearly all Christians', which, however, suggests that any belief in their being pagans cannot be so very widespread. We will return shortly to the interpretation of the responses to the statements about sexual urges.

An interesting parallel can be drawn between the results of this survey and those of an experiment carried out by Professor Eysenck and one of his collaborators. Eysenck writes: 'While there is little doubt that stereotyped attitudes play a part in the opinions of people, social psychology is in danger of developing stereotyped views about the nature of this concept of "stereotype".[11] Much of what is accepted on experimental evidence is in reality artefact produced by inadequate methodology.' He cites an American inquiry in which a hundred students were presented with eighty-four adjectives, with the request that they should pick out those characteristic of various nationalities. Considerable agreement was found among the answers – Germans are scientifically minded, methodical; Italians are artistic, musical; Negroes are superstitious, lazy; Americans are industrious, sophisticated; Turks are cruel, sensual. Eysenck doubted the interpretation of this experiment, so he and his collaborator repeated it in Britain. The results were almost identical. However, they introduced a new element, requesting the subjects to write reports about their own reactions to the tasks they had been set. This showed the material in a very different light: 19 per cent of the subjects had in the first place refused to do the test, declaring it to be 'meaningless' and 'impossible'. Of those who agreed to do it, 59 per cent considered the tasks meaningless as they did not know any representatives of these various nationalities; they pointed out that only long residence in a country could enable one to say anything worthwhile about people there, and that even then 'people everywhere differ among themselves'. But if the experimenter insisted on setting them such a task, then they had to fall back upon what they had seen at the pictures, read in the newspapers or heard vaguely in conversation; they were fully conscious that the qualities thus attributed to the various nations probably portrayed nothing but bias and preconceived notions.

The same applies, in principle, to many of the replies to the racial attitudes survey. Time and again respondents mentioned their limited acquaintance with coloured people, emphasizing that they could generalize only from that experience and that they realized it was limited. Faced with the statements about the supposedly stronger sexual urges of coloured people many people gave it their assent, saying 'at least, that's what I've heard'. Others said they had heard this said, that it might be true, but that they had no knowledge of it and would not therefore list this as one of the statements with which they agreed. Clearly, there is very little difference between these two reactions, and had the response rate been even double what it was it would have been totally illegitimate to accept this as proof of the existence of a stereotype.

We can accept the view that there are many current beliefs about coloured people of an irrational character, totally lacking in scientific validity, without conceding these notions the status of stereotypes. They are received ideas, things people heard said and to which they give a certain credence, but hardly anyone lives his life by them. The pragmatic attitude of finding out what people are like before judging them is far too strong for that. Received ideas about the cultural poverty of coloured peoples form part of our own society's heritage of ideas but they are not articles of faith.

Later on we examine the data from the attitude survey in greater detail and consider the extent to which the response rates given in Table I need to be modified on account of the tendency of some subjects to assent to contradictory propositions. For example, of the ten people in every hundred who endorsed the statement that coloured people are innately inferior, no less than six agreed that they were 'just as good as us when they have the same training and opportunities'. It would appear that the proportion of the British population who consciously subscribe to doctrines of racial superiority is certainly less than 4 per cent, while the proportion who are prepared to translate such opinions into active hostility is very much smaller still. Among certain minorities, like adolescent ne'er-do-wells, racial intolerance may be general, but the behaviour of these groups poses problems of a different order.

This discussion has in no way been intended to dispute the utility of psychological models in the study of prejudice. The theories outlined have revolutionized our understanding of why particular sorts of people express prejudice and how social factors can influence its manifestation. But they do not, and cannot, explain how it is that some situations occur in which even the least prejudiced of people discriminate against minorities. The authors of *The Authoritarian Personality*, for example, could not see social factors as having any but a secondary role. Speaking of the consistency with which the same ideas and modes of thought reappear in the discussion of one topic after another, they say: 'Since no such consistency could conceivably exist as a matter of sociological fact, we are bound to conceive of central tendencies *in the person* which express themselves in various areas.'[12] We shall hold that on the contrary it is equally valid to approach these problems from the sociological standpoint regarding personality variables as purely circumstantial factors. This approach might suggest that there is a consistency in patterns of behaviour that could not conceivably exist as a result of personality organization and must be the result of central tendencies in the social structure. But this would be equally misleading were it offered as a complete explanation.

CHAPTER III

EXPLAINING DISCRIMINATION

Sociology is not interested in proportions, but in relationships and the
behaviour that results from them.   T. H. MARSHALL[1]

COMPARED with the advances recently recorded by psychologists
the sociology of race relations has made very little progress in
recent years. This is due in part to the popular demand that the
sociologist shall write in simple prose and eschew technical terms which
the lay reader considers unnecessary. While it is easy to sympathize
with this view and to smile at the high casualty rate in the jargon-
mongering of any science struggling for its independence, the appeal
to popular language can have pernicious effects. The field of race
relations is beset with common usage concepts, like 'race' and 'colour',
which have no analytical value for sociology, and while the writer who
binds himself to them may be able to produce illuminating journalistic
interpretations of the situations he studies, his theoretical contribution
will be meagre.

Many people still have difficulty in seeing that 'race', as a biological
concept, has nothing to do with race relations. Men do not react to the
physical characters of strangers — texture of hair, pigmentation, eye
folds, broad- or narrow-headedness, etc. — but according to the social
significance that is placed on these characters. Where two groups are in
conflict we sometimes find that they interpret the same physical or social
characters in opposite fashion. Sociologically speaking, they are responding in similar fashion to a situation which is construed differently
according to the side from which it is approached. As many writers on
this subject have observed, a man's skin colour is noticed only in
certain situations. A very rich or powerful coloured man may not be
thought of as black, whereas a lighter-skinned man in a menial occupation may be. The ways in which 'race' and 'colour' are perceived vary

more bewilderingly than the biological phenomena, and it is only by getting away from the simple images of popular speech and examining some of the anomalous and apparently trivial features of relations between varying sorts of groups that we will be able to uncover the sociological dynamics.[2]

The celebrated natural historian Buffon once remarked that 'there are in nature only individuals. Races, orders, classes, exist only in imagination'. In one sense this remains true, but we may add that in nature there are also relationships and it is these which science seeks to uncover. Partly for the reasons just discussed, and because of the inescapable political importance of racial conflict, sociologists have often failed to specify the scientific problems presented in such situations. These appear to be of two kinds. In the first place the sociologist is required to show how discriminatory behaviour is entailed by the structure of group relations — why it is, for example, that Negro sharecroppers are brought into conflict with poor white tenant farmers or sharecroppers rather than with, say, white railway employees. In the second place, having shown how wider social factors structure the situations in which actors are involved, he has to explore the implications of this structure for the participants. The structure does not limit the choices open to the actor but it sets upon each its price; some courses of action are rewarded, others are penalized. People may also succeed in manipulating the structure and in presenting in a favourable light actions which might otherwise evoke disapproval. The relations between these different components of social situations have not received the attention they deserve.

The most influential of contemporary theories of discrimination is undoubtedly the Marxist. According to one of its best expositors, Oliver Cromwell Cox, 'race prejudice is a social attitude propagated among the public by an exploiting class for the purpose of stigmatizing some group as inferior, so that the exploitation of either the group itself or its resources or both may be justified'.[3] The classic statement of this thesis is probably Lenin's, in *Imperialism, The Highest Stage of Capitalism*, where he argued that imperialist policies divided the working-class movement, buying off opportunist workers by offering them some of the fruits of colonial exploitation. He quoted from a letter to Karl Marx in which Engels wrote:

> The English proletariat is becoming more and more bourgeois, so that this most bourgeois of all nations is apparently aiming ultimately at the possession of a bourgeois aristocracy and a bourgeois proletariat *as well as* a bourgeoisie. For a nation which exploits the whole world this is, of course, to a certain extent justifiable.

Writers of this school frequently present race prejudice as something consciously and deliberately fomented by the ruling class to distract the workers' attention from their legitimate grievances. White workers in the American South who seek to defend their privileged position in the labour market against Negro competition are represented as having either been bought off by the capitalists or been duped by them. The real source of their frustrations lies in the ruling class. Whereas Dollard's followers might hold that the employers are part of the white society with whom the workers identify themselves and which they are reluctant or afraid to attack, Marxists would hold that this is an illusion sponsored by the capitalists to prevent the proletariat — white and black — from joining hands. From a Marxist viewpoint much of what ordinarily passes as irrational attacks upon a scapegoat is therefore seen as the direct exploitation of subordinate classes by those in power. The same tactic is also sometimes attributed to financial barons who hide their operations behind a smoke-screen of allegations that Jews are responsible for all economic ills. A Hitler or Bismarck may aid his rise to political power, or his retention of it, by building up a scapegoat and encouraging the population to vent upon it their frustrations. Discrimination against Jews has also been represented as a sort of status-exploitation, for by excluding Jews from clubs and residential neighbourhoods the ruling classes may heighten their own exclusiveness and give themselves a feeling of moral superiority. Anti-Semitism can then be used as a mask to hide their class privileges. The encouragement of anti-Semitism has been further represented by

Communists as a device for exciting people's aggressive instincts in preparation for an eventual onslaught on the Soviet Union.

The claim that race prejudice is deliberately manufactured often betrays a striking credulity. It may well be that to describe relations between Englishmen and Nyasalanders as those between European and African *races* is to conceal political and economic elements important to an understanding of the relationship. It may be that statements such as 'Orientals only need a handful of rice a day to live on' are the rationalizations of people with a vested interest in the prevailing state of affairs. But this does not mean that such descriptions or statements are conscious products; nor would such an assertion be in accordance with Marx's own more scholarly views. Marx held that man's position in society determined his consciousness of the things about him, so that his response to a particular situation is not to be seen as the expression of individual will but as a reaction conditioned by circumstances. If he acts contrary to the forces determining that situation he will be made to suffer for doing so, and will be brought back into line. Paramount among the factors which in this way determine the general course of conduct is that of class interest. People are united by common interests and separated from others by conflicting interests. These interests are conceived as fundamentally of an economic character, the possession of power being desired as a means of exploitation. The members of particular classes come into conflict when their interests are opposed, and they are bound to do so, for if they do not defend their interests they disappear. The objective interest of the class determines its members' perceptions of the situations they are involved in, but only a select few are aware of this. The production of doctrines which further class interests is thus rewarded by the structure of society.

Some writers have advanced a simplified version of the Marxist theory, holding that the major factor in racial conflict is economic competition. For example, Carey McWilliams writes:

Profit or advantage is the motive force of group discrimination. The conflict between groups, as the conflict between individuals,

42

is not rooted in nature; it is not due to a difference in race or culture. On the contrary, it is an aspect of the competitive social order in which we live.[4]

By viewing competition in isolation from its political context this theory fails to account for certain features of discrimination; in particular, it does not explain why some sets of people — like Scotsmen and Quakers — may be particularly successful in certain fields without being perceived as competing groups. Nevertheless, both business men and trade union leaders are often inclined to explain racial friction almost exclusively in these terms. The Marxist regards racial discrimination as the outcome not of prejudice but of class interest; left to themselves the proletariat would unite, but the policies of the ruling class operate to maintain customary distinctions between them. Race prejudice flourishes in so far as it works in this direction.

Social life is highly complex, its various elements such as beliefs, institutions and modes of production, being interdependent. None of these elements can be maintained unless it harmonizes with the others. Marxists, however, attach a special significance to the role of material conditions in social development which makes theirs fundamentally an economic interpretation of society. Material conditions are said to determine the beliefs and institutions of the historical period, but seeing that changes in the modes of production cannot take place unless the other circumstances are favourable it is difficult to see how this one aspect of development could ever be proved to underlie the others. Even given that material circumstances exercise a limiting influence upon the development of new ideologies and customs, it is clear that there must be considerable room for trial and error and that there are problems in this sphere which cannot be solved in terms of a simple economic determinism. Secondly, the claim that British workers' perceptions of coloured immigrants are determined by their class position is of little assistance; most of them seem to have no difficulty in distinguishing between the immigrants as people and as possible competitors for employment. Relations between immigrants and working-class Britons present many features which are not adequately explained by their being forced into the categories of class perception.

A third and, from our standpoint, most important criticism of the Marxist theory is that it ignores important aspects of inter-group relations by concentrating upon political features and upon the circumstance of exploitation. Thus Cox says that race prejudice is propagated for the purpose of stigmatizing some group as inferior and facilitating its exploitation. He differentiates between race prejudice as directed against Negroes in the United States, and anti-Semitism which he considers a form of social intolerance, 'a reactionary attitude supporting the action of a society in purging itself of contrary cultural groups'. Our point is that whatever the political functions of prejudice, it is other things too: it is a psychological, sociological, geographical, historical phenomenon — and much else besides. If the view that economic relations determine all other aspects of social life be rejected, then these other aspects must be studied in their own right and the political functions of prejudice will be the main focus of interest only for the student of political science. Arguments about what prejudice 'really is' are futile. If prejudice against Negroes fulfils the same personality functions as prejudice against Jews, then the psychologist may treat them as similar for his purposes. Historically viewed, hostility against either of these groups serves different political ends at different times and in different places. Thus it is the social scientist's selective interest in particular problems which decides which aspects of events he will concentrate upon and how he will conceptualize them.

How far have recent studies of race relations in Britain contributed to the elaboration of a more satisfactory model for studying discrimination? Not to any very great extent. Only within the last few years has there been an appreciable coloured population in this country and patterns of inter-group relations are only slowly emerging. Because the situation was a new and fluid one without any obvious parallels in the literature, and because of the attractive sophistication of recent American research into the sociopsychological aspects of prejudice, some of the British research workers were not always sufficiently aware of the difference in the context of relationships in the two countries. In the United States relationships between whites and Negroes have

44

been formalized to a far greater extent than in Britain, and the concepts used in American research reflect this pattern. The application of these concepts to the British scene led to the presentation of an over-formalized picture. Furthermore, if the investigators were to obtain the confidence of their informants, as it was very necessary they should, they had to identify themselves personally with many of the coloured immigrants' criticisms of the whites, and thus they tended to see the British situation through coloured eyes. These two factors led them to make an extensive and sometimes uncritical use of the concept of prejudice and to neglect the more teasing problem of discrimination. In contrast to this we may cite the view of Dr Ruth Landes who brought to her observations a perspective based upon lengthy personal acquaintance with the interracial situation in North and South America. Dr Landes has expressed her doubts about whether the concept of prejudice as it is understood in the United States is at all applicable to the British scene. In a paper read before the Royal Anthropological Institute she said:

I grew increasingly sceptical of the generally accepted concepts, as applied to Britain, of Prejudice, Tolerance and Acceptance. I felt that something else was going on, and it could be grasped if the right questions were asked. 'Prejudice' seemed to muddy up the approach; it didn't seem a helpful assumption in Britain. In America I knew it for a sociological reality, distinct and compelling. An organized system of values and conduct, it was taught by the authorities, forcefully and lucidly. It was a machinery that regulated thought, impulse and act, private and public, wherever the races met. No American was ever in doubt about its proprieties. Consequently the individual could choose between two positions respecting it: he could support it or he could fight it, and in either case he was oriented knowingly. But in Britain I see no such orientation. In this sense, therefore, I would say there is no prejudice. I could say there is a certain confusion, particularly on the part of the coloured immigrant. This is because he guides himself in terms of a logic of complete acceptance, whereas Britons act in terms of a much more limited acceptance.[5]

Coloured people are perfectly acceptable in certain relationships but excluded from others, whereas in a variety of intermediate situations reactions towards them cannot easily be predicted. A theory which helps to reveal an underlying consistency in this apparent disorder has been advanced by Dr Kenneth Little in *Negroes in Britain*, a study centred upon Cardiff and carried out during the Second World War. Dr Little emphasized as important influences upon British attitudes both the extent of popular ignorance about the colonies and their inhabitants, and the carry-over of historical attitudes reaching back to the days of slavery. Economic competition was an important factor underlying conflict, but 'social prejudice' constituted a subtler problem:

> Some English persons believe that they will jeopardize, if not lose, their social status in the eyes of their friends and acquaintances by association with a coloured person. Their reaction might be likened to the hesitation shown by a fashionable or highly class-conscious person at being seen talking in public to someone who is shabbily dressed or who speaks with a socially unacceptable accent. It may aptly be described as colour-class-consciousness.[6]

In another publication he added:

> Skin colour has a definite significance for many English people, a darker complexion making a person socially less acceptable ... Though many of the individuals concerned may lack personal prejudice, they feel that their social reputation will be jeopardized if they are known to have coloured friends or acquaintances. To introduce a Negro into their social circle would cause embarrassment ... 'Colour' has the same socially inferior connotation as English spoken ungrammatically, or without the 'correct' accent, or of wearing a muffler instead of a collar and tie.[7]

The great advantage of this hypothesis is that it makes allowances for differences in situations and the way they are defined. It helps us to understand not only why everybody disapproves of the coloured stowaway but also why all sorts of people are only too flattered to be introduced to the Indian Maharajah or the African chief whose title and genealogy ensure him an upper-class status. It suggests one reason why people are more ready to associate with coloured men at work than at home. Dr Little never developed this line of argument as he might have done, but important supporting evidence is furnished by Dr A. T. Carey in his book *Colonial Students*, especially in his analysis of what he terms 'colour tax'. Because of the social disapproval of coloured lodgers a landlord tends to accept them only when there are no white people willing to pay the price asked for the services in question. The coloured student has either to pay more than the white student if he is to secure comparable accommodation, or to accept inferior facilities, which means paying more for them than they are really worth. The difference between the market value and what the coloured man has to pay is the 'colour tax'; it measures social disapproval in material terms. 'From the point of view of the landlady', Carey writes, 'colour tax represents compensation for possible loss of social prestige; from that of an observer, it is an undesigned and unintended consequence of a social structure whose system of values includes the premise that association with coloureds is synonymous with "low class" and generally disreputable behaviour.

The strength of the 'colour-class-consciousness' hypothesis is that it is independent of psychological assumptions, and interprets behaviour solely with reference to features of the social system. Avoidance of coloured people is a pattern of behaviour entailed by the objective features of situations in which other courses of action would evoke social disapproval.

However, it may be maintained that in explaining the behaviour of particular actors psychological factors may be very relevant and that a conclusion like the one just stated fails to indicate why a dark skin colour should be associated with low social prestige. Dr Little approached this latter problem historically. The identification of coloured people with the lower social classes he saw as an outcome of the Industrial Revolution, which upset the existing class structure and made members of the middle classes anxious about their position, and consequently ready to assert their claims. Educational standing and the mastery of genteel ways acquired new significance as class indicators.

The coloured man had none of these: 'his only qualification was his blackness, the former label of "slave", and its other associations. He fitted in, therefore, only on the bottom rung of the social ladder to elevate those hardly less lowly placed than himself and to become thereby the recipient of social attitudes whose basis was class as much as race.' But the historical approach is not related satisfactorily to the sociological hypothesis, and indeed the two seem to be regarded as alternative hypotheses, for in summarizing his conclusions Dr Little writes: 'English people display for the most part tolerant if somewhat prejudicial ideas regarding coloured people', and continues: 'nevertheless, it is a moot point whether the unfavourable reactions promoted do not in fact derive from the implications of other attributes, in particular of the low status of coloured persons in Britain … '

Dr Carey also tackled the problem of relating conventional attitudes towards coloured people to the way in which social situations are structured, but his approach inclined to the psychoanalytic. Impressed by the strength of 'the stereotype of the Negro as a sexually uninhibited and highly potent being', he concluded that 'in view of the highly emotional character of certain reactions towards Negroes … an interpretation of prejudice solely in terms of fears about loss of social prestige seems incomplete'. To complete the picture required some incursion into psychology. Dr Carey accepts the Freudian view that all actors experience an internal conflict and that there must therefore be an out-group to give social expression to the division within the actor himself. Out-groups are necessary, if only to enable members of the in-group to deal with conflicts, internal and external, without wrecking their own group. Therefore, says Carey, groups are likely to be formed wherever there are stable means of distinguishing people; and where actors are allocated to groups on a basis of external appearance people will be more aware of differences between the groups and less aware of differences within them. Furthermore, landladies' attitudes towards colonial students are to a large extent based on the sentiments they believe others hold about coloured people, which supports the view that the sentiments of an individual towards a particular group

are determined less by his knowledge of that group than by his interpretation of the sentiments prevalent in the social atmosphere that
surrounds him. Why then should the Negro be associated with low-
class and uninhibited behaviour? The out-group, he suggests, represents
threats to the in-groups's values, particularly to middle-class standards
of conduct in matters of sex. Thus the popular view of the Negro as a
sexually highly potent and at the same time uninhibited being apparently includes elements of envy as well as of hostility and fear. This
has the advantage of allowing people to ascribe to others a kind of
conduct that is at once desired and socially disapproved.

Dr Carey's attempt to link the psychological and sociological factors
betrays him at times into portraying social patterns as the product of
individual sentiments — a thesis contrary to his own theoretical position. Thus he writes of colour tax as 'an unintended and undesigned
consequence of the general prevalence of colour prejudice' in a context
where 'prejudice' appears to denote individual dispositions. Again, he
concludes that 'any sociological interpretation of prejudice must begin
by asking why the potential fund of hostility existing in all societies is
so often directed against those of another race ... ' In this respect his
argument resembles that of Mr Richmond discussed earlier, in seeing
personality forces as the dynamic and social factors as dependent
variables on the lines of the 'pipe and tap' analogy. It is open to the
same criticism as is his; it underestimates the extent to which
hostility shown towards coloured immigrants is not displaced but direct
aggression in that it is a rational response to certain kinds of situations.
Furthermore, where is the evidence that English people suffer so much
more from insecurity and frustration than nations which show little
racial prejudice? If the evidence is lacking, a case must at least be stated
to show that such nations are displacing their aggressions in other ways.

Psychologically oriented writers have tended to see social patterns as
the outcome of individual dispositions. Marxists, on the other hand, see
the individual's sentiments as determined by his class position.[9] In
criticism of both of these schools we have held that the psychological
individual and the sociological person are two aspects of the same actor
viewed from different standpoints, and that as no one can observe the

same object from two different standpoints simultaneously a synthesis of the two aspects is not possible. But so radical a separation is acceptable only in analysing such social phenomena that can be treated as if they were static. In fact, no one social situation is identical with another: they follow like the sequence of still photographs that make up a cinematographic picture, each one very slightly different from the preceding. Relations between racial groups are always changing though the norms governing conduct may appear to shift only slightly. The process by which the norms change is the cumulative interaction between the attitudes, values and beliefs of the actors on the one hand, and the inherited way of life on the other. Sociologists see this not as the nineteenth-century opposition of 'the individual' and 'society', but as the interrelation of custom (or culture) and social organization (or social structure). As Professor Meyer Fortes observes:

> Custom is the behaviour that is standardized, expected, and often enforced in a particular situation in the community. Social organization is the system of arrangements by which the social relations of the members of a community with one another are regulated and ordered. Social relations are in part matters of custom, and custom is in certain respects the expression of social organization.[10]

The rights and obligations of the person are a feature of the social structure, but they are defined by custom, and custom changes. Thus in discussing popular attitudes towards coloured people we shall treat them not as the opinions of an aggregate of individuals considered as if they existed in isolation but as objective characteristics of custom.[11]

By recognizing the cultural features of the British scene as phenomena in their own right we are enabled to consider the historical influences explicitly. The association between a dark skin colour and the 'lower classes' is to be explained by reference not to unconscious psychological factors (though these may have supported it) but to the way British people have in recent years learned to regard strangers and colonials. Virtually all Britons, even those who are very friendly and those who are very hostile towards coloured immigrants, share many common views about the newcomers and about the appropriateness of certain kinds of behaviour involving members of the two groups. There are many who are personally most well disposed towards coloured men, but are nevertheless repelled by the idea of their marrying English or Scottish girls. The ordinary Briton may feel superior, but this is because he also feels under some sense of obligation to the colonial whom he regards as a pupil or ward of the mother country. Often, again, he is sympathetically disposed towards anyone with a dark complexion because in other countries they are treated in a fashion that conflicts with British ideals of personal liberty. There may be an element of hypocrisy in some of these varied attitudes but that does not make them any less influential. Stemming very largely from the biological and political doctrines of the nineteenth century, British views about interracial behaviour constitute a distinct cultural tradition.

In the following chapter we outline the way in which this tradition has developed, afterwards examining how far the view of the coloured man differs from conventional images of the stranger. We next attempt to use this material for developing a theory to account for some of the vagaries of British conduct towards coloured people and in this light consider case material describing group relations in different circumstances.

Part II

THE UNSPOKEN LANGUAGE

CHAPTER IV

CHANGING CONCEPTIONS OF THE COLOURED MAN

London abounds with an incredible number of these black men, who have clubs to support those who are out of place; and in every country town, nay in almost every village, are to be seen a little race of mulattoes, mischievous as monkeys, and infinitely more dangerous.   PHILIP THICKNESSE, 1788[1]

COLOURED people have been resident in Great Britain for over four hundred years. From the middle of the sixteenth century onwards many Negro slaves were brought to England to serve as domestics in fashionable households. Before the end of the next century their numbers were sufficient to attract attention, though few people seem to have thought their presence undesirable. After Lord Mansfield's famous judgment in 1772 that slavery was not 'allowed or approved by the law of England', which brought to an end the importation of coloured servants, the number of coloured residents seems to have gradually declined.[2] From the end of the eighteenth century onwards there was a small but steady flow of coloured visitors, both seamen and youths who came to study. There were also occasional visits from colonial potentates who stayed for shorter periods and had little contact with the populace.

The changes which the popular image of the coloured man has undergone illustrate well how one group's view of another is not just the outcome of its experience of the other group. The European conception of the coloured man has been powerfully influenced by the views Europeans have in different epochs held about the nature of human society. In the diaries of Columbus and the accounts of subsequent explorers the life of coloured inhabitants of distant lands is often described in glowing terms, but with the opening of the romantic era in the eighteenth century we find these observations moulded into a powerful myth: that of the noble savage.[3] The belief that man was naturally good was allied with the view that the ills from which he

55

suffered were the result of a faulty organization of society and could be remedied by its reform. It was developed not so much by the rationalist philosophers bent on the transformation of existing institutions as by their more romantic followers. In France the image of the noble savage acted for a time as a spur to political agitation, but after the Revolution its appeal rapidly dwindled away. The upholders of tradition, like Samuel Johnson — who was nevertheless most attached to his Negro servant and opposed to slavery — were less impressed by 'cant in defence of savages'. In eighteenth-century Britain we hear little of supposedly significant biological differences between Negroes and Europeans. Several writers comment on the inconveniences of importing Negro servants when they were all too apt to desert their masters and, living often on their talent as beggars, congregate in the St Giles' district of London, but the breath of racialism is absent from their arguments.[4] The Master of Magdalene College, Cambridge, must thus have enunciated a widely held opinion when, in his 1784 sermon before the University, he referred to 'a great part of the human race, whose external complexion indeed is different from our own, but who are formed of the same blood with ourselves; who partake in common with us of all the faculties, and all the distinguishing excellencies of our nature'.[5] The West Indian planters and their friends disputed this view, however, and a division of opinion soon became apparent.

Sir John Hawkins, the sea captain, was the first Englishman to take part in the African slave trade. In 1562 he plundered the coast at Sierra Leone, carrying off three hundred Africans for sale in the West Indies. In subsequent years many English ships were engaged in transporting the unhappy creatures across the Atlantic. But, terrible as were the sufferings of the slavers' human cargo, this traffic proved more degrading to those who practised it than to its victims, and it provoked a powerful revulsion of sentiment among the public at home. When an enterprise is as lucrative as was this it never lacks apologists, for the merchants' profits benefit a large section of the nation and forge a chain of vested interests. From the closing years of the eighteenth century onwards the theory that Negroes were fundamentally different from Europeans appears to have obtained steadily increasing support, spurred on perhaps by the champions of the West Indian slave-owners. Members of the opposing party defended their views with vigour. As Sir Richard Burton said of the African, 'before the Wilberforcean age, he was simply a negro. That trade which founded Liverpool, and which poured five million pounds of sterling into the national pocket, marked him to the one class a Man and a Brother, to the other a Nigger.'[6] Pro-slavery speakers and writers were only too ready to argue that the Negro was an inferior being, fit only for slavery and to spread the claim that he was better off under a Christian master than when left in his native ignorance. Many of them alleged that Negroes were an inferior species of mankind, and though their propaganda on this issue may have converted few it probably sowed doubts in many people's minds.

The struggle for the abolition of the slave trade was won in 1807, but slave-holding remained legal in the West Indies and other British territories overseas for another twenty-six years. For the anti-slavery enthusiasts the Negro was often an object of philanthropy and an innocent whose cause was to be defended against colonial administrators and merchants. This conception has been fostered down to the present day by some missionary bodies. It was believed by British Protestant missions that Africans lived in complete ignorance of God, of His grace, and His expectations of humankind. Western Europe's sense of superiority was well expressed in the original version of Bishop Heber's famous missionary hymn 'From Greenland's icy mountains':

> What though the spicy breezes
> Blow soft o'er Java's isle,
> Though every prospect pleases,
> And only man is vile ...
> The savage in his blindness
> Bows down to wood and stone
>
> Can we whose souls are lighted
> With wisdom from on high
> Can we to men benighted
> The lamp of life deny?

Missionaries helped create an image of the Negro as lacking any culture or religion of his own. If this view was accepted there could be no point in attempting to understand his way of life. Though it was conceded that some non-Christian peoples, like Indians and Arabs, had religions and civilizations of their own, the Negro was thought to have nothing — except what the whites were so kind as to give him.

An impression of the contending factions and their arguments can be gained from Carlyle's essay 'The Nigger Question' published anonymously in *Frazer's Magazine* for December 1849 and the reply it elicited in the next issue. According to Carlyle the ex-slaves rejected the good Scots doctrine of the duty of labour. He resented their opportunity — as he imagined it — to live in comfortable idleness. 'To do competent work, to labour honestly according to the ability given them; for that and no other purpose was each one of us sent into this world.' The typical Negro was 'poor Quashee ... a swift, supple fellow; a merry-hearted, grinning, dancing, singing, affectionate kind of creature, with a great deal of melody and amenability in his composition'. As a result of emancipation 'we have few black persons rendered extremely "free" indeed. Sitting yonder with their beautiful muzzles up to the ears in pumpkins ... while the sugar-crops rot round them uncut'. Carlyle railed against 'Exeter-Hallery and other tragic Tomfoolery' — Exeter Hall being where the abolitionist groups held their meetings. The Negro was the lowest of the human species and Carlyle's advice to him was: 'I do not wish to see you slaves again: but decidedly you will have to be servants to those that are born *wiser* than you, that are born lords of you; servants to the whites, if they *are* (as what mortal can doubt they are?) born wiser than you?' The abolitionist writer in his rejoinder rejected Carlyle's gospel of labour and the appeal to the more brutal features of the natural world: humanitarianism was nobler than strife. He regretted that the essay would give aid and comfort to American slave-owners and stigmatized it 'a true work of the devil'.

In the middle years of the nineteenth century interest in colonial expansion died down and was not revived until the last three decades, when the scramble for colonies on the part of Britain's continental competitors, and increasing pressure from the manufacturing interests, induced successive Governments to accept responsibility for further overseas territories. The growth of imperialist sentiment was rapid and with it was associated a belief that the English were by nature a people destined to rule the inferior races of the world to the benefit of both parties. This attitude became particularly evident at the time of the Boer War and in the self-satisfaction of the jingoist era — 'We don't want to fight, but by Jingo! if we do! We've got the ships, we've got the men, we've got the money too!' Despite the economic and political strength of England during this period it is nevertheless improbable that the imperialist philosophy could ever have taken such a hold upon the nation's mind had it not been for the development of certain anthropological and biological doctrines. No longer was it generally believed that coloured people 'partake in common with us of all the faculties and all the distinguishing excellencies of our nature'. Out of the great flow of new ideas and fumbling scientific advances the circumstances of the time selected those that were politically convenient and stretched them to justify actions motivated by narrower interests. In the course of time science overtook these convenient errors and exaggerations, but not until they had served the ends of their generation.

Anthropological theories — particularly those about the origins of mankind — have exercised considerable influence upon European attitudes towards coloured men. In earlier centuries the Judeo–Christian belief that all mankind were descended from an original pair, Adam and Eve, was a tenet of faith. Those who questioned it were persecuted. In the seventeenth century Dr Lightfoot, a Vice-Chancellor of Cambridge University, had concluded that 'man was created by the Trinity on October 23rd, 4004 B.C., at nine o'clock in the morning'. And as late as 1886 we find Sir Samuel Baker, the African traveller, concluding that there could be no doubt as to the rapidity with which races became differentiated, for the difference between Englishmen and the Africans of the White Nile must have been the work of only 5870 years. The men who founded the Ethnological Society in London in 1843 inclined to this view. The moving spirits among them were Quaker philanthropists who had supported the anti-slavery cause. In the controversy of the day they were known as monogenists, opponents of the polygenists who believed that the different races were of separate origin. The polygenist theory was an old one, and, despite attempts to suppress it, had been gaining ground in scientific circles with the discovery of previously unknown peoples in the New World and in distant territories. In the controversy over the abolition of slavery in British colonies, and the parallel movement in America leading, in 1861, to civil war, frequent appeal was made to the conclusions of anthropology. This led to the secession from the Ethnological Society in 1863 of a group of members favouring the polygenetic view; they believed that anthropology ought to make its contribution to political discussion by popularizing its discoveries. Its president launched this new venture with an address on 'The Negro's Place in Nature', in which he concluded that the Negro was a species distinct from the European; that the analogies were far more numerous between the Negro and the ape than between the European and the ape; that the Negro was inferior intellectually to the European; that the Negro race could only be humanized and civilized by Europeans; and that European civilization was not suited to the Negro's requirements or character. In England, a tremendous outcry greeted the publication of this address, but in the southern states of America its author's views received a warmer welcome.[7]

Yet the anthropological dispute was stillborn, for in 1859 Charles Darwin had published his epochal work *On the Origin of Species by Means of Natural Selection; or, The Preservation of Favoured Races in the Struggle for Life*, which demonstrated the role played by the selection of the fittest in the process of natural development. His work showed that the monogenists were hopelessly wrong in believing that man appeared perfected and complete, a species distinct from all others; the polygenists were equally wrong if they insisted that man emerged in several places in several distinct forms. Darwin established a new monogenist theory according to which man was the ultimate product of a long and incalculable process of steady differentiation. Twelve years later, in the *Descent of Man*, Darwin dealt with selection in the human species. The races of man presented him with a problem he found puzzling, for, as he says, they differ in every physical character in regard to which individuals are known to vary. He made no attempt to classify races and added that we have no right to give names to objects which we cannot define. Nevertheless, he recognized considerable differences that had been 'nearly constant for very long periods of time' and realized that they could not be the product of environmental factors. Finally, he came to the conclusion that human differentiation was due to sexual selection, the choice by men and women of partners whom they found most to their taste.

Darwin's discoveries were given to a world already prepared for them by developments in geology and kindred sciences, and by the writings of Herbert Spencer, 'the great expounder of the principle of Evolution', as Darwin called him. The doctrine of natural selection as the driving force behind development supplied the missing foundation stone for the theory of evolution. The first edition of Darwin's book sold out on the day of publication and had an instantaneous effect. Its theory accorded with the temper of the age in several respects. Darwin's inspiration came from Malthus; applied in the biological field, the postulate of continual struggle fitted the facts better than it had in the sphere of population studies. In the early decades of the industrial era, when some made fortunes and many starved, life must often have seemed an extended combat. Years before the *Origin of Species* Tennyson had described nature as 'red in tooth and claw'. Thus the extent to which the new ideas upset religious susceptibilities should not be allowed to obscure how much they harmonized with other tendencies. The more progressive writers on social questions soon saw their problems in a new light and promptly began trying to translate Darwin's formulations into a law of social development, earning for themselves the name of 'social Darwinists'. Unfortunately, they lacked their master's scientific caution. One of the first was Walter Bagehot who published in 1873 a book entitled *Physics and Politics, or Thoughts on the Application of the Principles of 'Natural Selection' and 'Inheritance' to Political Society*, in which he argued that 'those nations which are strongest tend to prevail over the others; and in certain marked peculiarities the strongest tend to be the best'. Shortly afterwards the Austrian sociologist Gumplowicz applied the same argument to the struggle for survival between races, and the tide of similar writing flowed in such spate that Benjamin Kidd's *Social Evolution* (1894), a work of slender merit, sold a quarter of a million copies. Three aspects of this trend of thought deserve particular attention: the search for the unit of social development, which many found in the concepts of nation or race; the attempt to apply to this unit the theory of the selection of the fittest; and the impact of evolutionary teaching upon the political scene.

One of the first writers in modern times to produce a serious argument for regarding race as the determining factor in human affairs was Count Arthur de Gobineau, a French aristocrat, who in 1853 published his *Essay on the Inequality of the Human Races*. There he contended that the decay of societies was not due to religious fanaticism, corruption, licentiousness or luxury, as was popularly supposed, but that it was caused by the mixture of races and adulteration of good stock by the admission of inferior elements. His book was almost completely ignored in France until after 1900, though it began to attract attention in Germany when after the war of 1870 its author became a friend of Wagner's. Gobineau's emphasis upon race as the major factor in selection was continued in Germany by O. Ammon and in France by G. B. de Lapouge. They came to constitute the 'anthroposociological' school which vainly measured vast numbers of people in an attempt to uncover physical variations between nations, between town- and country-dwellers, and similar groups. Though less inspired by poetic romanticism than some other contemporary writers on race they spoke constantly of the Aryan race as superior, and frequently implied or openly asserted the correspondence of their Aryan with the tall long-headed blond. An American authority's judgment upon the anthroposociologists' contribution is much to the point. He wrote: 'If they had deceived themselves only, little harm would have resulted. But they greatly strengthened doctrines upon which have been based pernicious forms of racial arrogance in Germany, England and the United States. They assisted in the inflation of Teutonic chauvinists and Pan-

Germanists; they lent aid and comfort to Anglo-Saxon imperialists; they gave a sense of moral righteousness to the spirit of racial intolerance.'[8]

At the same time developments in genetics led to a growing emphasis upon the stability and continuity of races and species as opposed to earlier views of their mutability and change. In Germany, August Weismann developed his theory of 'the continuity of the germ plasm' according to which the characteristics of a race or species derived from an immortal germ plasm handed on from generation to generation. This theory, it has been said, harmonized very well with the claims of Prussia and the German aristocracy, and reinforced political theories of racial hegemony.

Towards the end of the century the educated public in Western Europe and America became increasingly concerned about race, and the word attained general currency in writings on many topics. One book which attracted considerable attention was Charles H. Pearson's *National Life and Character* (1893), the burden of which was the inevitable rise of the prolific black and yellow races (the former 'very little raised above the level of brutes', the latter for the most part 'of such secondary intelligence as to have added nothing permanent to our stock of ideas'). The same assumptions about race underlay its frequent use as a synonym for nation, and this misleading term was introduced into historical and literary writings. Matthew Arnold, for example, wrote at length about Celts and Teutons, about Hellenism and Hebraism, and though he did not himself subscribe to the racialist philosophy his use of this terminology helped to make such ideas respectable.[9] In Britain the racialist fallacy attracted little attention after the opening of the century and many liberal writers exposed it fairly effectively. In the United States, however, it survived for another two decades, bolstered by the fear that the nation was admitting immigrants of poor stock whose assimilation into the population would lead to a general deterioration. Thus in 1917 we find Maddison Grant, himself a charlatan but shielded by scientists of repute, writing *The Passing of the Great Race*, in which he affirmed that 'the result of the mixture of two races, in the long run, gives us a race reverting to the more ancient, generalized and lower type. The cross between a white man and a negro is a negro; the cross between a white man and a Hindu is a Hindu; and the cross between any of the three European races and a Jew is a Jew.' The same sort of nonsense was peddled by another popular writer, Lothrop Stoddard. Many serious and sensible people were influenced by alarmist talk that America was receiving only Europe's cast-outs and by fear of the 'yellow peril' in the Pacific. Thus Jack London, normally considered a progressive writer, feared the threat of the coloured races and strenuously advocated racial assertiveness on the part of the whites.

The original social Darwinist argument was that the members of human societies competed with each other, resulting in what was termed intrasocial selection. This doctrine, which was accepted by T. H. Huxley and survived in the work of Benjamin Kidd, was soon abandoned by the majority of scholars. Spencer gave it up, and adopted the alternative view, known as intersocial selection, according to which different societies struggle against one another for survival. Prince Peter Kropotkin in his valuable book *Mutual Aid as a Factor in Evolution* (1902) reminded the public that Darwin himself had said that in numerous animal societies the struggle between separate individuals is replaced by co-operation in order that the community may survive. The same was true of human societies, and those of his followers who ignored co-operation within species had failed to understand either animal or human society. Sir Francis Galton and Karl Pearson, both influential writers, inclined to the same view and opposed the intrasocial theory of selection. Where Spencer, the pacifist and internationalist, shrank from applying his intersocial analysis of selection to international relations, Karl Pearson knew no such inhibitions. A fiery controversialist, pupil of Galton and professor at London University, Pearson held that 'the nation was a unity evolved by the struggle of one living type under the same laws as applied to other phases of life' and that thus 'the theory of the state became biological'. In a booklet called *National Life from the Standpoint of Science*, published in 1901 and reprinted several times, he held that from a genetic standpoint Negroes were poor stock, and 'if you want to know whether the lower races of man can evolve a higher type, I fear the only course is to leave them to fight it out among themselves'. Moral principles might be no guide, for 'when the struggle for existence between races is suspended, the solution of great problems may be unnaturally postponed'. Speaking with the authority of a Fellow of the Royal Society he assured his listeners that 'the scientific view of a nation is that of an organized whole kept up to a high pitch of internal efficiency by insuring that its numbers are substantially recruited from the better stocks, and kept up to a high pitch of external efficiency by contest, chiefly by way of war with inferior races ... ' He asserted that the 'continual progress of mankind is the scarcely recognized outcome of the bitter struggle of race with race' and developed a most ingenious defence of colonialism. According to Pearson it was advisable to prepare for times of national crisis a reserve of brain and physique; 'such a reserve can always be formed by filling up with men of our own kith and kin the waste lands of the earth, even at the expense of an inferior race of inhabitants'.

Pearson's mentor, Sir Francis Galton, was a man of very different temper. It was he who first pointed out that men are not all alike in their mental traits but that abilities often run in families. Until Galton demonstrated this it had been held that ability was developed by education and hard work alone. Galton went further, however, and argued that heredity must be taken account of in human affairs. Just as horse-breeders achieve the best results by mating horses of good stock, so we should encourage the best elements in the population to have large families and sterilize defectives so as to prevent their passing on undesirable traits. He became the founder of what has been termed, perhaps a little kindly, the science of eugenics. In Galton's life and work we see the terrible tragedy of a great man of science, himself kindly and of humane disposition, who opened up a new field of inquiry and who yet was unable to distinguish between what was science and what was only a reactionary philosophy of social change. The acceptance by a man of his intellect and integrity of the thesis that different races could be distinguished and compared with one another, and his use of a mock statistical technique to this end, must have assisted considerably the propagation of racialist theories. Galton confidently proposed that couples of 'worthy' genetic qualities should be given special allowances to help them at the start of their married life and to enable them to have many children. Today, the naivety of such a proposal is startling: could any acceptable procedure ever be devised for selecting such persons? Furthermore, the advance of knowledge in the field of genetics since the rediscovery in 1900 of Mendel's work has shown that the breeding of good stock is not so simple as Galton imagined. Though his scientific contributions have been absorbed into the growing stream of knowledge the ideological movement Galton inspired has retained a special following.[10] As Lancelot Hogben wrote in 1937, 'the eugenic movement of this country has always been an organization of a small section of the professional class with a strongly conservative bias directed to restrict the further extension of educational opportunity'. Prominent eugenists have repeatedly equated good genetic stock not only with particular races but with particular classes within our own society. According to this view the middle class is a group of persons of hereditary ability superior to that of the working class. Such is the opinion not only of many amateurs but of at least two geneticists of international reputation. Opposed to such an interpretation, however, is a growing school of thought which lays emphasis upon the superior development of many hybrids — hybrid vigour or heterosis it is called — and which holds that existing techniques are inadequate for measuring interaction between environment and the 'genotype'.

The social Darwinist idea that the nation could be regarded as an organism gave a new sense of purpose to the study of history. For if evolutionary processes were at work in the rise and decline of nations, then an understanding of the fore-ordained course would give man greater control over his condition and a new realization of how far he could change his circumstances. Thus Sir J. R. Seeley, Regius Professor of Modern History in the University of Cambridge, concluded that the key to the understanding of modern times was the expansion of England decreed by 'a Providence which is greater than all Statesmanship'. Summing up his argument, he wrote: 'The peculiarly English movement, I have urged, has been an unparalleled expansion. Grasp this fact, and you have the clue to both the eighteenth and the nineteenth centuries ... this formula binds together the past of England and her future, and leaves us, when we close the history of our country, not with minds fatigued and bewildered as though from reading a story that has been too much spun out, but enlightened and more deeply interested than ever, because partly prepared for what is to come next.'[11] The strength of his insistence upon the inevitability of the process expressed in his 'formula' (itself an expression scarcely beloved of historians) may be seen from his statement 'so decided is the drift of our destiny that after we had created one Empire and lost it, a second grew up almost in our own despite'.

Belief in the inevitability of evolutionary processes coloured many political arguments of the time. It led Herbert Spencer to deny the possibility of securing social progress by direct remedial legislation and to assert that society must wait for the automatic working of the general laws of development. It led another history professor, John Adam Cramb, to argue that big wars were better than small wars. In a series of lectures given in London during the South African war, Cramb pictured the state — in true Hegelian manner — as 'the embodiment in living immaterial substance of the creative purpose of the race, of the individual and ultimately of the Divine'.[12] From this it was but a short step to pronounce that imperialism 'is patriotism transfigured by a light from the aspirations of universal humanity ... in a race dowered with the genius for empire, Imperialism is the supreme, the crowning form, which in this process of evolution it attains'. War was therefore, according to him, 'a phase in the life-effort of the State towards completer self-realization, the perpetual omnipresent strife of all being towards self-fulfilment'. In the South African war two principles equally lofty and impressive were at stake, 'the dying principle of Nationality and the principle which, for weal or woe, is that of the future, the principle of Imperialism'. This struggle was 'the first war waged by the completely constituted democracy of 1884', and its end 'the larger freedom, the higher justice, a war whose aim is not merely peace, but the full, the living development of those conditions of man's being without which peace is but an empty name'. In the professor's system of doublespeak war was peace, and there were many listeners only too ready to adopt his casuistry. But this was

not the end of the lecture-room Vulcan's revelation; he went on —
'looming already on the horizon, the wars of races rise portentous,
which will touch to purposes yet higher and more mystic the wars of
empires'.

The views of Pearson, Seeley and Cramb may have been extreme
but they are not to be discounted, for they represent the strongly
nationalist sentiment of an age that was itself extreme. The arguments
of the liberal writers who pleaded for internationalism today seem
almost self-evident; their force and significance can be appreciated only
when set against such a background.

The trains of thought that sprung from the writings of Darwin and
Spencer combined to elevate the jingo spirit that lasted from the late
1870s for over twenty years, and which reached its peak in the orgiastic
exuberance of Mafeking night, a display that shocked people who were
not otherwise prudish. Englishmen began to take a vicarious pride in
the achievements of their colonial heroes, and there grew up a new
literature of military adventure. This movement reached its peak in the
popularity of Rudyard Kipling's works with their glorification of
action, and in the elevation of the author to a popular idol of prodigious
influence. This rise of a popular electorate underlined the crudity of
such trends and called forth the cheap newspaper press. Harmsworth's
Daily Mail, founded as 'the embodiment and mouthpiece of the
imperial idea', reached the unprecedented circulation of a million copies
within five years. A similar appeal to racialism was made by Horatio
Bottomley's *John Bull*. Many people believed that the general egocen-
tricity of the era was justified by the pseudo-biological doctrines that
were then gaining credence, and one critic suggested that a new
beatitude had been incorporated in the national religion: 'Blessed are
the strong, for they shall prey upon the weak.' An authority upon the
history of this period, Professor Langer of Harvard, concludes that
though economic factors were important in the growth of imperialism,
'the prevalence of evolutionary teaching was perhaps crucial. It not
only justified competition and struggle but introduced an element of
ruthlessness and immorality that was most characteristic of the whole
movement.'[13]

The men who worked in the colonies, administrators, merchants and missionaries, were regarded with increased respect by those who stayed at home. In the colonies a pattern of segregation inevitably developed. The Europeans lived in their own communities, and when they came into contact with the natives they did so as superiors dealing with inferiors. The difference lay in their superior knowledge and skill, not in their racial origin. But these two very different qualities were easily identified with each other and it was thought that a European was superior simply because he was a European, without reference to differences of education or the fact that the measure of ability was the purely European technological standard. People at home came to take it for granted that the European gave orders to colonial peoples and that this was the proper pattern of relationship. The influence of the missionaries worked in the same direction, for they were thought of as taking benefits to the heathen, doing for them things they were unable to do for themselves — superior to them as the teacher is to the pupil. To rouse interest and support among church people missionary bodies glamorized the work of their agents and described native life in horrifying terms. The reports of administrators, merchants and missionaries brought home to the public the technological backwardness of the colonial peoples, and, as civilization was so often equated with machines and material benefits, this reinforced the image of the coloured man as uncivilized.

One of the minor consequences of the 1914-18 war was the recruitment of coloured colonials for manning merchant ships and for service in labour battalions. Several hundreds settled in Britain after the cessation of hostilities, and it is from this time that the growth of coloured communities in Liverpool and Cardiff dates. This story has been told at length elsewhere. It remains only to observe that relations between whites and coloured men in this country appear to have reached their nadir of disharmony in the inter-war period. Unemployment in the seaports was largely responsible for this; but the racialist doctrine of earlier years may have sharpened the conflict and canalized local resentment.

Lest it be thought that the fallacies of bygone days have here been credited with overmuch influence in the shaping of contemporary attitudes, we may perhaps consider a particular example. While conducting research into colonial immigration but a short while ago the author heard it asserted several times that if a white woman has intercourse with a coloured man there is always the danger that any baby she may bear, perhaps years after the incident in question, may prove to be coloured. Miss Webster has independently reported the occurrence of this belief among Oxbridge students. A significant number of people either believe it to be true or give it credence. Here, surely, is an irrational piece of folklore. Yet we find that Darwin in *The Variation of Plants under Domestication* (1868) gave countenance to such a belief. It was supported by the case of a mare that had been mated with a zebra-like animal, giving birth to a hybrid with faint stripes. Later the mare was mated with a black Arab stallion and bore three foals which had the same stripes as the hybrid, though more markedly. Their colouring was thought to have been due to the first mating, though biologists now know that the stripes were inherited from one of the mare's remote ancestors.[14] Nevertheless, the belief persists. English sheep-breeders will not allow a pure-bred ewe that has once been mated with a ram of another breed to remain in the Flock Book. The prevalence of such an idea long after it has been disproved in biology is but one example of the tenacity of the scientific myth when it appears to lend authority to a socially convenient belief. Much of today's racial folklore is in fact the science of a century ago. Contemporary discussions of the 'half-caste' often echo the faulty generalizations of the Anthropological Society of 1863.

In the 1930s hostility towards coloured people was associated chiefly with competition for employment as seamen. After the outbreak of war there were jobs for all, and people's minds turned to other things. The assistance in the war effort given by the colonies to the mother country led to colonial immigration similar to that during and after the First World War, though this time it was on a considerably larger scale. West African seamen settled in the ports, and from the last years of the war up to 1951 there was a steady trickle of one or two hundred stowaways per year. Then from 1948 onwards began a stream of immigration from the West Indies, from Jamaica in particular. This movement was composed mostly of ambitious workers whose employment opportunities had been restricted by the rapid growth of the labour force in their home countries and the curtailing of migration to the United States. They have received a more friendly reception than many earlier groups of migrants, due in part to the public's new awareness of the political importance of race relations. This improvement in attitudes has been buttressed by increased economic security and may also be in part the fruit of the earlier swing towards idealism reflected in the League of Nations. The League was the expression of a changed outlook upon international affairs and it encouraged the growth of a new attitude towards the technologically backward nations of the world.

In the absence of any thorough study of the development of British thought on the question of relations with coloured peoples our judgments must remain superficial, but certain characteristic features may be discerned. The role of political factors is one of the most noticeable. First, the struggle over slavery split public opinion into two camps, driving the parties into extremist positions. Later, in the age of imperial expansion, we see Britons caught up in new relationships with which is associated the belief in their moral and social superiority over their subjects — a belief which has not been reflected to any appreciable extent in the views of European nations possessing no colonies. Then, as imperialism gives way to an era of what the French have called 'decolonization' and former colonies regain their independence, the association of a coloured skin with a subject status is weakened. Indians and Pakistanis are not now regarded in the same way as twenty years ago, or as Nyasalanders or Gambians are today. Yet to suggest that changes in public opinion are determined by political developments is to oversimplify matters, for the pace of political change is itself regulated by the climate of public opinion in the countries concerned.

The part played in the formation of British attitudes by the results of scientific inquiry and a rational search for the truth about racial characteristics does not at first blush appear impressive. Doctrines which suited particular interests have been inflated and conclusions too hastily drawn. But special pleading about racial superiority has not enjoyed more than temporary success. The racialists once based their arguments upon differences in cephalic index or the supposed degeneracy of the Negro; now that these claims are generally discredited they fall back on such sophisticated discoveries as variations in the distribution of the sickle-cell trait, or dilate upon the African's 'addiction to female circumcision'.

The question which chiefly concerns us here, however, is the influence of these beliefs upon relations between whites and coloured people. At no time since 1772 have the courts considered the rights of coloured residents to be in any way different from those of whites, or their obligations to be in any way less. But during the imperialist era coloured men were conventionally regarded as having special claims upon British benevolence and were not thought to be entitled to the same social privileges as white men. In the sphere of custom they were not accorded the same rights, nor were the same obligations demanded of them. In this sense they were socially subordinate. Now the old pattern of conduct is dissolving. While coloured men may still be prepared to tolerate patronage in certain situations they resist it bitterly in others, and Britons recognize that the old norms are no longer always appropriate. This uncertainty about the relevant norms of conduct must occupy a central place in any analysis of the present situation. We shall therefore consider the general function of norms in interpersonal relations before examining the factors which hinder the establishment of an unambiguous code of behaviour.

CHAPTER V

THE ARCHETYPAL STRANGER

The Englishman is no missionary, no conqueror. He prefers the country to the town and home to foreign parts. He is rather glad and relieved if only natives will remain natives and strangers strangers, and at a comfortable distance from himself.   SANTAYANA[1]

THE network of relations that constitutes a society is maintained by a series of common understandings as to the rights and obligations of the persons who occupy positions in it. Social life can be seen as a sequence of relationships, each of them being defined by the rights and obligations of the parties to it. Norms of conduct in given situations may be explicitly stated in the law of the land, or they may be implicit in the conventions to which people subscribe. The continuance of social life is dependent upon the members of society observing these norms, and sanctions are applied against those who infringe them. Seen from this standpoint, strangers are people who do not know or will not accept the norms. They are not necessarily foreigners: the small child, the wealthy eccentric, the tramp, the village idiot, are all strangers to their society in that their behaviour cannot be predicted with any certainty, and the various informal pressures that usually produce conformity are not effective in their case.

In some societies little is left to chance, and a high proportion of the norms by which conduct is to be regulated are made explicit; if not in the constitution or the law, they are explicit in public discussion and are consciously taught to newcomers. Britain would appear to be one of the countries where the reliance upon implicit norms is particularly high. Britons, naturally, would be the last people to be aware of this, but American sociologists accustomed to the strenuous efforts made to turn varied groups of immigrants into patriotic American citizens are frequently impressed by this aspect of British social life. Thus Professor

George C. Homans: 'Any society rests on a set of unstated assumptions, British society more than most: that is, indeed, its strength.'[2] Dr Ruth Landes has similarly observed: 'Here in Britain you have an ancient community of populations bound by the wordless understandings that root in long acquaintance ... in Britain people do not have to be told how to act, for they are as one long habituated organism.' A French correspondent, M. Pierre Maillaud, was struck by the way these 'wordless understandings' preserved the multitude of social degrees in pre-war London Society. 'It requires', he wrote, 'Napoleonic attention to details, such as the tone of voice, the practice of cordial detachment, the suitable dose of affability, and perhaps the proper variations of address to animals, from hunter to Pekinese.' It may be, as Dr Landes suggests, that the more deeply rooted and isolated a society the less need there will be for its norms to be rendered explicit.

These implicit notions about the proper way to behave, about the unannounced rights and obligations of people in particular positions, constitute the unspoken language of British social life. The Briton expects those with whom he has dealings to observe an unspoken code. If they deviate from it he will indicate by his tone of voice, a change of manner, or by silence, that he is unhappy about the turn events are taking, and if the other party fails to take the hint the relationship may be broken off. But Britons are aware of these codes more in breach than in observance: a variety of things are 'not done', but there are relatively few positive regulations. Reliance upon the unspoken language is greater in the social classes near the top end of the scale than at the bottom. In the higher classes, acceptance of certain tacit standards is such that the minor social neglect of a person of inferior prestige can be a powerful sanction, and the more urgently someone seeks to climb the scale the more sensitive will he or she be to such pressures. In the rougher working-class districts, like those in the neighbourhood of the docks, sanctions of this sort have little effect and the resort to violence or the support of the police is far more frequent as a means of obtaining conformity. Thus it is easier for the stranger to gain acceptance in the lower social categories. The extent to which he is accepted by groups higher up the prestige scale will be partly dependent upon the extent to which he has learned their ways and is therefore subject to their controls.

The statement that a stranger may more readily gain acceptance at the bottom of the class hierarchy is subject to several qualifications. There is often a greater show of unfriendliness towards foreigners among the least favoured classes. It is as if, feeling no cause to be proud of their class, they identify themselves the more strongly with the nation of which they are members. Thus George Orwell wrote: 'The famous "insularity" and "xenophobia" of the English is far stronger in the working class than the bourgeoisie ... Nearly every Englishman of working-class origin considers it effeminate to pronounce a foreign word correctly.'[3] This difference, however, probably reflects not the underlying disposition of members of varying social strata so much as ideals of good manners and the fashionable value of cosmopolitanism. It is our impression that working-class people more readily manifest hostility towards coloured people but are more readily induced to abandon it. If an upper-middle-class person dislikes coloured people he will conjure up an inexhaustible store of arguments to justify his views, for they do not spring to the same extent from a lack of information as is likely to be the case with a worker. It is indeed surprising how little insight some intelligent people have into their attitudes on this topic, as may be illustrated by the number of times people who express opinions indicative of antipathy towards coloured people finish by affirming that they themselves are not prejudiced. Miss Webster cites just such a case. An Oxbridge graduate was telling her how, when he was about to take a bath and realized that it had been used immediately before by an African:

A feeling of revulsion swept over me. I didn't want to take a bath where they had bathed. I couldn't help looking for the grime from their bodies; of course, there was none. I am not conscious of any race prejudice in me, but there is something mysterious that sets them apart from us; they are different. I have many good Negro friends, but there is always this mystery.

Why does a young child notice the difference in the street, and laugh and stare? It is because there is a very deep difference between them and us. It is not a social but a psychological thing.

I am completely unprejudiced.

From such evidence no one could assert that the man was prejudiced, but the final emphasis upon his innocence suggests an unwillingness honestly to face up to the question which is by no means atypical.

Englishmen are known all over the Continent for their insularity, for their supposed belief that they have little in common with other nationalities; indeed, even in English the word 'alien' has a most peculiar and distasteful flavour. 'British' and 'foreign' appear to be two of the chief categories of the Englishman's thoughts and of his understanding of the world. All people who are not Englishmen are foreigners, and though foreigners may differ among themselves the most important thing about them is their common characteristic of foreignness. Most nations make a similar distinction and it may be doubted whether the English are so much worse offenders than others, but foreign commentators seem to be unanimous on this point and we cannot be judges in our own case. Professor G. J. Renier, in his amusing yet serious book *The English — Are They Human?* had no doubt about it: 'everywhere', he wrote 'patriotism implies an instinctive feeling of group consciousness. Only in England does it rest on a judgment of value.'

It might be thought that the Briton's conception of Britishness is an implicit belief in the inheritance of certain biological characteristics, and opinions can fairly easily be collected which appear to support this view. Salvador de Madariaga, for example, avers that 'the English instinct of co-operation operates within a well-defined group which is no other than the race. This is, at bottom, the true meaning of the expression "British Empire"'. Such explanations, fruit of the glib racial theories of the last century, reflect but a superficial view of one aspect of an intricate cultural complex. How the various features of national behaviour cohere is a problem on which we have little information, but it may be suggested that one of the factors underlying this insularity is the dependence upon the unspoken language. An actor must be able to interpret the other person's behaviour and convey his own sentiments fairly easily. This intuitive understanding of others is achieved more rapidly when a man is dealing with people who have a background similar to his own; he knows that they will see matters in much the same light as he does and that there is no great danger of his being misinterpreted. This illuminates the reserve shown in dealing not only with strangers of another nation but of another social class. As an Oxbridge girl student said: 'The people who don't speak King's English don't want to mix with us; they stick together. It's natural for us to associate with members of the same class; it's *more comfortable*. For instance, I am in a group where everyone's parents also went to the university — we have the same kind of background.'[4]

Part of the complex which chimes in with this is the Englishman's emphasis upon cultural identity. Margaret Mead came to the conclusion that 'The English regard culture as something that is very slowly and painfully learned, and while less often critical of foreigners than Americans are, do not expect them to become English.'[5] Enlarging upon this distinction between the two nations, she wrote: 'The Americans see the world as man-controlled, a vast malleable space on which man builds what he wishes, from the blueprints he has drawn, and when dissatisfied simply tears the structure down and starts anew.' On the other hand, 'the British see the world as something to which man adapts, in which he assumes no control over the future, but only the experienced foresight of the husbandman or the gardener, who plants the best seed and watches over the first green blades'. This attitude is a key to the Englishman's understanding of himself. He holds that a man's cultural heritage makes him what he is: that a man's integrity consists in being true to his own background.

In the English world-view culture is always the culture of a particular nation or group, a way of life that can be learned only over two generations and not something — like the 'American way of life' or the French conception of civilization — that can be taught. The Englishman is irritated rather than flattered by imitation. In the colonies he tends to think that 'the bush native is a good fellow', and displays the utmost scorn, and indeed sometimes hatred, of the 'savvy boy', the 'babu' and

77

the mission boy who assumes English ways; like 'half-castes', they are neither the one nor the other. He is more impressed by the African in a colourful and flowing native robe than in morning dress. He tends to respect the African who professes Islam more than the one who says he is a Christian. What is sometimes thought to be racialism is primarily people's reluctance to try making friends outside their immediate circle. The Englishman in some distant colonial station thinks it only natural that he should keep his club for himself and his fellows, as a place where they can relax in security and where there will be none of the awkwardness which would be inevitable if they were to admit people who do not share their assumptions. This self-segregation on the part of the Europeans has been bitterly resented because, in the colonial situation, it is their group which controls the centres of power and constitutes the social elite. The outcome has been such that one writer at least has claimed that 'it could be said without too much exaggeration that the fear of strangers lost Britain its Asiatic empire'.[6] The present writer himself, both in West Africa and in Britain, has been impressed by the same phenomenon: it is not so much that the Briton is against the coloured stranger but that he prefers to avoid him if this can be done without its being too obvious. This attitude both springs from the valuation of cultural identity and is justified by it. The Englishman desires above all to retain his own cultural distinctiveness and judges others in terms of his own proclivity.

It is hard, very hard, for a stranger to become British. Feeling that the objective is virtually unattainable, and in any case scarcely desirable, Britons do not encourage him to try. The new norms of conduct round which the stranger would have to rebuild his personality were he to mix with complete freedom[7] are the less easily apprehended because they are not made explicit; and for this very reason Britons are not sufficiently conscious of them to be able to teach them. Learning to be British is made even more difficult in that the newcomer has to learn, not a uniform national culture, but a class and perhaps regional culture appropriate to his position, which, while sharing many common features with the other sub-cultures, differs from them in important respects.

Though there are no sharp dividing lines in Britain between one class and another, and although many people pass from one class to the next, the characteristics of class remain relatively constant. For most English people the notion of class is an important reference group enabling them to 'place' others, for though they may have widely different ideas about how many social classes there are, and how they are composed, most people think of themselves as belonging to a particular class, while nearly everybody tends to place most of his or her acquaintances in some class. Even if the individual is not sure about where he himself belongs in this scheme he is confident about the class membership of many other peoople.[8] Writers sometimes determine class membership by reference to a man's income, which is a convenient method because it enables sharp if arbitrary lines to be drawn and everyone to be fitted in. Yet more important perhaps than how much money comes in is the way in which it is spent, for class differences are more than anything else cultural differences. Many factors go together: income, occupation, education, residence, style of dress, accent, recreation, and so on almost inexhaustibly. Each social class has to some extent its own culture, that is, a way of life with its sets of values, customs and equipment. Cultural differences, for example, between the working and middle classes are very evident in the sphere of child rearing. Working-class parents are almost invariably much more permissive in allowing their children to have their own way in food habits, cinema-going, staying up late, playing unsupervised in the street, etc. Middle-class parents are usually more ambitious for their children and consequently demand more from them; toilet training is achieved earlier and a stricter discipline maintained over a much longer period. Such differences, of course, are not a matter of arbitrary custom but are related to the material situation of the two classes. Working-class homes usually offer less opportunity for the children to play indoors; both parents may be out at work so that their opportunities for controlling the children are more limited, while the children become economically independent at an earlier age. Similarly there are class differences of an ideological character which are associated with different customary practices and which serve to justify

79

them. There are numerous middle-class norms defining the proper behaviour towards working-class people which are quite often made explicit in such expressions as 'you don't argue with a tradesman', 'you should never be rude to a servant because he or she cannot answer back'. Comparable working-class norms are less frequently made explicit because so many of the English working class outwardly accept the middle-class ideal of conduct as valid for themselves also. A notable instance of this is the working class acceptance of the 'gentleman' ideal; many are prepared to accept orders from a person conventionally regarded as a gentleman, where they are resentful of being ordered about by someone whom they consider no 'better' than themselves because he has grown up with a background similar to their own. This phenomenon, however, is not always more than skin deep. The dominance of middle-class conceptions is such that working-class people are apt to pay lip service to them whilst continuing to follow implicit norms of a different kind in their everyday life.

That people can climb from one social class to another does not necessarily weaken class differences and may indeed strengthen them, for the socially ambitious person strives to obtain the distinguishing characteristics of people in the higher class, and when he has 'arrived' he is apt to draw the line all the more sharply between those who have these characteristics and those who do not. Thus opportunities for climbing may only increase social selectiveness. Class-cultural distinctions of this sort are still of very real importance in English life. Professor Alan S. C. Ross, who touched off the recent 'U–Non-U' controversy, declared that upper-class people are so sensitive to accent that 'one single pronunciation, word or phrase' will suffice to brand an apparently upper-class person as of socially inferior birth. Movement down the scale can be equally difficult. In *The Road to Wigan Pier*, George Orwell, an Old Etonian, described how he grew up to believe that the lower classes smelled, and how as a young man he felt a physical repulsion from them. To expiate his own feelings of guilt Orwell lived for some time as a tramp and as a lodger in a miner's cottage, 'but though I was among them, I was not one of them', he wrote, 'and they knew it even better than I did ... It is not a question of dislike or distaste, only of difference, but it is enough to make real intimacy impossible.' Such 'muscular-curate efforts at class-breaking', he concluded, were 'a serious mistake. Sometimes they are merely futile, but where they do show a definite result it is usually to intensify class-prejudice.'

Even if it is rarely so marked as this nowadays, class-consciousness undoubtedly exercises a strong influence upon English behaviour. The acceptance of such differences and the alienation of the self from persons placed in other categories, is, from a comparative viewpoint, a remarkable feature. To take another example: in Sweden class differences have been so reduced that it is extremely difficult for even a native-born Swede to guess the occupation, income or family background of a chance acquaintance, for there are scarcely any characteristics of accent, clothing or taste to give him a clue. Thus the Swedish visitor to Britain a few years after the War who examined the furniture displayed in the cheaper shops was apt to protest that it was all in shockingly bad taste and that people should never be allowed to sell such stuff. The population should be educated to buy goods that were aesthetically more attractive. The Englishman never saw it that way. He would argue that people should buy what they liked and that working-class people found such furniture aesthetically attractive. Underlying such an argument, of course, is an acceptance of class differences and a denial of uniform cultural standards. In some fields, such as education and housing, class differences have of late been much reduced by the spread of reformist middle-class standards backed by long-term economic considerations, but nevertheless English people appear still to accept such differences more readily than most nations.

Are differences of colour comparable to 'class stigmata' — as Orwell thought? Later on we shall contend that Britons view coloured men as strangers to their customary way of life in much the same way as they might view members of a different class, and parts of our analysis will be just as applicable to relations between classes as between any social groups which are regarded as possessing different rights and obligations from members of the actor's own group.

It has also been suggested that while the concentration of people in urban centres makes it easier for people to find some niche for themselves, the anonymity of city life makes it difficult for the newcomer to build up a truly satisfying role. Thus Geoffrey Gorer in his recent book *Exploring English Character*, writes: 'my impression is that, though life in big cities everywhere has a tendency to isolate, and, as it were, atomize the inhabitants, this process [of loneliness] has been carried further, and for more people, in England than in any other country with which I am familiar.' The newcomer who comes to live in a village is immediately forced into intimate relations with his neighbours and with those with whom he trades. The newcomer who settles in a large town often establishes only restricted relations with those about him. His landlady is interested in him only as a lodger or tenant, the shopkeeper is interested in him only as a customer and not as an individual, and so on. This characterization of city life can easily be overdrawn and is certainly untrue of many neighbourhoods, but recent studies in urban sociology[9] have demonstrated that a large proportion of city-dwellers are afraid that their neighbours should learn anything of their private affairs. Many of them insist 'I keep myself to myself' or 'I don't believe in visiting between neighbours', stressing what they do or do not 'believe' as if this were a religious creed. It may be, as Thorstein Veblen suggested, that because of the emphasis upon showy possessions in contemporary civilization people save their best things for their public appearances and prefer to conceal the consequent shabbiness of their domestic life. While from another viewpoint it may be seen as expressing people's need to maintain control over the relationships they make when they have the freedom to choose their associates.

Mr Gorer sees the question in terms of his theory of the English character, which he thinks potentially very aggressive but held under strict control. The desire not to be overlooked derives from the widespread use of deprivation as a childhood punishment. Shyness is a type of fear — fear that strangers will treat one with contempt because of one's own shortcomings — or fear that strangers will corrupt or contaminate one, either by undermining one's self-control, or by undermining one's social position through association with people who are 'no class'. Why, he asks, should this be so when strangers are often tongue-tied but seldom wounding? Presumably because people project on to others the wounding intentions they might have if they did not keep a strict watch upon themselves. It is fairly commonly remarked that people anxious about maintaining or improving their social position do not wish to be seen in the company of their inferiors. In societies where social status and race are closely associated with one another, such as in some West Indian islands, a coloured person of fair complexion may not like to be seen too often in the company of very dark-skinned people. Another respect in which strangers can be a threat is in connection with conventions of sexual behaviour. The Englishman is noted for attempting to minimize the role of sex because it is one of the major sources of conflict and disruption in social life. Mr Gorer says that more than half the population believe that a cross-sex friendship can be sexless ('platonic'), which would surely not be echoed in many other societies. Social life can be more sedate when people tacitly agree to tone down the sexual element; yet this arrangement is threatened when foreigners appear who do not play the game, but set out to attract the women and force the men to compete in what they had previously thought their private preserve. English men and women regard foreigners of the other sex as more exciting than their own compatriots. As individuals they are less conscious of English inhibitions in the company of strangers and often choose foreigners — either when at home or abroad — as partners for their own extra-marital adventures.

In a passage referred to in the previous chapter, Dr J. H. Robb suggested that the characteristics ascribed to an out-group are likely to reflect some of the needs and repressed wishes of the hostile individual. The images which Britons with strong colour prejudice have of the coloured man have not yet been the subject of scientific scrutiny, but if Mr Gorer's theory is correct then it may well be true that the Negro is the white man's fear of himself. The Africans' and West Indians' capacity for letting themselves go, which some British people see as their most engaging characteristic, is for others one of the snares of the Devil. As Dr Landes said: 'I suggest that the Englishman's remarkable stress on personal and social discipline is deeply affronted by the Negro's incomprehensible and perhaps theatrical zest and spontaneity. To him this is possibly the most alien element of all, counting as irresponsibility and naked indulgence.'

These various considerations suggest that in Britain the coloured man is not seen as a different sort of being but as the furthest removed of strangers — the archetypal stranger. The same conclusion was reached by Dr Landes, who with a characteristic turn of phrase referred to the Negro as 'relegated to the far nether end of that great range wherein the Briton strings the places of all the non-Britons of the world'. This view is borne out by the ordinary Englishman's very uncertainty as to who is to be considered 'coloured' and who is not. Maltese immigrants in the East End of London, for example, are sometimes referred to as 'coloured'; so are Cypriots on occasion, though most people would never consider them so. The children of a mixed marriage are invariably considered coloured, for they are obviously in some way strangers. Thus even though it is a gross exaggeration one may quite seriously characterize English views on this subject in the frivolous phrase 'niggers begin at Calais'.

Norms of conduct towards coloured people usually differ from those of conduct towards other whites not in kind, but in degree. Some evidence to support this inference may be obtained from the results of our racial attitudes survey.

From the survey it transpires that individual Britons are simultaneously well disposed towards coloured people and yet prefer not to be too closely involved with them. The responses to selected statements set out in Table I showed a sharp distinction between the favourable and unfavourable propositions, and the pattern is repeated in other answers to this series of questions (see Appendix II). Answers to a question regarding the restriction of colonial immigration suggested that public opinion on this topic was more favourable than might have been expected in view of the numerous proposals that had been advanced in 1955 and 1956 for limiting the influx from the West Indies. Respondents were asked: 'Provided, of course, that there is plenty of work about, do you think that coloured colonials should be allowed to go on coming to this country?' — 72 per cent replied in the affirmative; 18 per cent were definitely opposed, and the views of the remainder could not easily be classified. Of those who were in favour of maintaining an open-door policy, nearly half emphasized the proviso as to the availability of work, or suggested that they should not be allowed to congregate in towns where there were difficulties in obtaining work. (The discrepancy between this response and the results of certain opinion polls is discussed in Chapter VI.) As illustrations of some of the factors which weighed most heavily with the persons interviewed, we may cite a few of their comments:

'Yes, if it helps break down this colour bar. It's only stirring up trouble to keep them away.' — Alcester housewife.

'We've been there long enough and exploited them, so now they come here — just like the Irish and others.' — Coventry machine operator.

'They fought for us, didn't they? They've as much right here as many of the Continental D.P.s we welcome with open arms.' — Alcester storekeeper.

'But there *isn't* enough work.' — Hawick housewife.

'It's *our* country.' — Alcester housewife.

The distinction between individual friendliness and an acceptance of social distance came out clearly from two questions about discrimination in housing. People were told: 'Sometimes landladies and hotels refuse to take in coloured people'; and were then asked: 'Is this right or wrong?' — 12 per cent replied, unequivocally, that they were right in doing so, though a study of the answers suggested that in just over half the cases respondents were expressing tolerance of the landlady's behaviour rather than agreement with it; 52 per cent considered that refusal was definitely wrong. Most of the remainder gave qualified answers, indicating that circumstances vary and that the landlady or hotel manager must be allowed some latitude to decide for herself or himself; she or he must take into account the feelings of other guests, the neighbours and so forth. Many people would clearly prefer separate facilities if these could be provided without infringing coloured people's rights or hurting their feelings; they realize that this would be extremely difficult. Those who replied that discrimination was unequivocally wrong were later asked: 'What if their business may suffer?' This question appeared to cause many of them some difficulty. A minority considered it irrelevant ('People come before money'), an imaginary fear ('This isn't true today as it used to be'), or a false distinction ('Why just them? Some Irish aren't fit to be taken in'). Rather more admitted that this was a very real difficulty, but the vast majority gave no clear reply; there seemed to be a tug-of-war between the feeling that it is unfair to exclude coloured guests without giving them a trial, and, on the other hand, the view that business is business, that other people must be considered, and that it is unfair to pass judgment upon landladies when there is a danger of their suffering on account of their adherence to a principle that bears so much less heavily on other sections of the community.

The other question ran: 'Many coloured people from the colonies have difficulty in finding lodgings or accommodation. Which of these three things do you think we should do to get over these difficulties?' The interviewer then mentioned three possible measures: 'Make it easier for them to get rooms in hotels and boarding-houses; ask more private people to have them stay in their homes; provide hostels for them.' An overwhelming majority favoured the third of these suggestions: 71 per cent naming it by itself, and a further 10 per cent in association with one or both of the others. The reasons people gave for favouring hostels tended to fall into three categories: some people thought separate accommodation was in the immigrants' own interests as they were happier together and were protected from some of the unfriendliness of the whites, whereas others favoured segregation in the interests of the white population as they thought it would avoid trouble, and because they would not have wished to have coloured lodgers in their own home; the third set of reasons did not imply the interest of either group but featured the view that separation was preferable because the two groups have different customs, food, habits, etc., so that domestic mixing would be bound to cause friction. In general, respondents found it difficult to resolve conflicting sentiments, in favour of mixing and of keeping separate, or of distinguishing between the circumstances in which the different courses of action were appropriate. Among the comments we notice:

'Build hostels in the same area and so have a coloured quarter — not ignoring them but being social too.' — Leeds joiner's mate.

'A small estate, perhaps, but not in a separate compound. They have their own ways and no bad thinking is created by different habits. Hostels get nearest to this — but don't have separation.' — Alcester hospital worker.

'They're happiest all together, though I wouldn't mind having a coloured man in my house. When my husband was abroad he looked for English families — I'm not contradicting myself am I?' — Ipswich housewife.

'There's some ill-feeling towards coloured people. It's better to have them on their own — like the Jews in London.' — Hawick tweed worker.

Taking all the answers together, we find that 22 per cent expressed definite opposition to any possibility that might tend towards segregation; 26 per cent favoured hostel accommodation as a temporary measure or in the immigrants' interest; while 45 per cent chose hostels for reasons which appeared either to suggest a preference for separation or an acceptance of it as a necessary consequence of cultural differences.

Evidence from other sources supports the same general conclusion, though there are indications that the degree of social distance whites feel from coloured people has been declining in recent years. Miss Webster administered a Bogardus-type social distance test to girl students at an Oxbridge college and a teacher training college. Certain differences between the responses of the two groups are apparent from Table II. The university women far more readily expressed willingness to marry Russians, Chinese and Indians. The teacher training college women were more ready to exclude entirely members of all groups, while the particular rigour with which they regarded the Russians and

Chinese suggests that the responses reflected political as well as racial attitudes. The university woman — as Miss Webster points out in a more detailed analysis of the results — indicated a much smaller degree of distance, but, where she felt some, rather than suggesting complete exclusion indicated a course that would enable her to avoid intimate relations with strangers. But the most striking feature of the results is the relatively slight degree of social distance expressed throughout the test, compared with the data obtained by Professor Eysenck[10] from an earlier investigation based on a sample more representative of the total population. We may recollect, however, that young women such as those questioned by Miss Webster, and the university women in particular, would be more susceptible than most to the public protestations of racial equality and to ethical considerations (as one of the university women remarked when handing in her card, 'I've been very Christian'). Moreover, the subjects were not personally acquainted with the problems upon which the test bears and were themselves inclined to add 'We've never really thought about it'. The results may therefore not be a good guide to how they would behave in practice. Nevertheless, if we allow for the political loading in the teacher training college students' responses about the Russians there is a clear distinction between the subjects' willingness to accept members of the European nations as relatives by marriage, and their unwillingness to do so in the case of the coloured nations. This distinction is reflected more clearly in Eysenck's data.

The Bogardus-type test requires modification for use in different societies as the expression of social distance varies. Professor Eysenck came to the surprising conclusion that his subjects at least were more ready to admit a stranger to membership of their club than to British citizenship. 'To us,' he writes, 'admission to citizenship and employment indicate a greater degree of acceptance than does admission to street or club.' This question merits further investigation as it is not clear how such a finding is to be interpreted.

It is likely that the coloured man would appear less of a stranger were British people better informed about the background and aspirations of colonial immigrants. A relatively high proportion — 35 per cent — of those interviewed had some connection, such as through friends or relatives, with one or more of the colonies and dominions. Yet no more than 36 per cent were able to give a rough indication of the difference between a dominion and a colony. After they had in all cases been told or reminded of this ('Dominions are countries like Australia and Canada which run their own government; colonies are to some extent dependent on Britain for their government'), 43 per

TABLE II

The Social Distance of Five Stranger Nationalities

	I would marry one		I would allow my brother to marry one		I would allow into my club		I would let live in my street		I would allow to be employed in my occupation in my country		I would allow to become citizens of my country		I would allow as visitors to my country	
	Oxb.	TTC	Oxb.	TTC	Oxb.	TTC	Oxb.	TTC	Oxb.	TTC	Oxb.	TTC	Oxb.	TTC
Germans	72	69	87	77	96	91	98	94	98	95	99	98	100	98
Russians	54	16	71	27	87	42	92	50	94	52	100	75	100	97
Chinese	18	5	41	21	88	58	96	76	98	83	100	97	100	99
Indians	28	12	47	29	88	72	95	82	98	91	100	98	100	99
Africans	14	11	31	27	82	70	92	80	97	90	100	99	100	100

Subjects: 100 women from an Oxbridge college and 204 students at a women's Teacher Training College. Responses have been reduced to proportions of 100; a few were indeterminate.

cent were able to name two or more colonies correctly; 19 per cent were able to name three or more. Of the names offered, nearly a third were incorrect, being for the most part names of dominions; 79 per cent were sure that we were doing things in the colonies 'to teach the people there to govern themselves', but many were unable to mention any ways in which this was being done. Education was instanced (usually in very general terms) by 40 per cent of respondents, missionary work by 15 per cent, and the improvement of health by 11 per cent. Only 7 per cent mentioned the extension of the franchise and the transfer of power to colonial representatives. Comments on the whole displayed a bland confidence in British beneficence, but some critical voices were raised:

'That's the cause of a lot of the trouble, social reform and education, so that they go off on their own.' — Alcester housewife.

'They come here for education, then go back home and kick up a row.' — Leith tram-driver.

'We like to think we are ... ' — Coventry metal worker.

'Supposedly — but can't say how. Teachers, doctors, missionaries, doing a lot of good and a lot of bad.' — Alcester farm worker.

It was noticeable throughout that the moral element was stressed more in the answers from Scotland.

The suggestion that in Britain the coloured man is regarded as the stranger par excellence may cast light on the problem of national differences in the reception accorded to coloured people. They themselves say that the French, Italians, Scandinavians and others do not regard them as being in any way peculiar. A typical remark is that of an East African student: 'I liked France very much and felt a load dropped off my shoulders when I arrived in Paris. Everyone treated me normally and I forgot I was coloured.' In respect of colonial policies it would be difficult to demonstrate that the so-called Latin peoples are more benevolently disposed towards their colonial charges than the British, while from the evidence available it is not likely that as individuals the Britons are so much more antipathetic. The cause for the coloured man's complaint may well lie in the British tradition of maintaining a greater social distance, and the appreciation of cultural distinctiveness. It is as if they conclude that because the coloured man has his own cultural identity so there must be a special way of behaving towards him.

After showing how social life is regulated in terms of norms as to the conduct appropriate in particular situations, we have in this chapter argued that norms relating to coloured people differ from the others only in degree and that they are consistent with other aspects of British culture. But to discover what the factors are which allocate the coloured man to the end position in the scale of strangeness we must pick up some of the threads from our earlier discussion of changes in the Briton's conception of his rights and duties with regard to coloured men.

CHAPTER VI

WHEN CUSTOM FAILS

On Man: You hold that to be right which is merely wrong made public, which clothes you in the shroud of custom as soon as you are born, nourishes, educates, brings you up, rules you, according to which you are held to be honest, strong, wise, of good morals; thus governed you live according to custom, but not according to reason.   CARL LINNAEUS[1]

CUSTOM, as the embodiment of the unspoken norms, tells people how they should behave in particular situations. It stipulates that persons falling into a given social category are to be treated in a specific manner; for example, it is customary for men to raise their hats to ladies though there are many other ways in which deference might be expressed. Custom clothes all our everyday activities; in many shops it is usual for the shop assistant to comment on the weather as a sign of concern for the customer, and a failure to do so may be unfavourably remarked. Even where relationships are governed by legal requirements – as with the bus conductor's right to demand the fare from his passengers – the interaction between the two parties is moulded by purely conventional expectations as to how the other will behave. Any distinctive role in society is defined by prescriptions as to how people should behave towards the person in question and what conduct they should expect from him. No social category can retain its distinctiveness unless such norms are maintained.

Relationships with members of a particular social group may be regulated by special norms. Thus in the American Deep South a Negro visiting the house of a white man is expected to go to the back door. The coloured people know what to expect and what is expected of them in return. At the other extreme there are countries like Hawaii and Brazil where members of racial minorities are treated in almost the same way as everyone else: conduct is regulated by the same norms as govern a person's relations with people of his own group. It would appear that the position in Britain used to have many elements resembling the first of these situations. The special norms did not support any extensive system of discrimination, but pictured the coloured man as a colonial ward — a British subject in training and not a mature citizen. The position today has moved much closer to the second situation in which there are no special norms for behaviour towards coloured people. This is not meant to imply, however, that there is any necessary transition from the first type of situation to the second; a reversal of the trend is always possible.

According to the old norms, Britons, as a more advanced nation, were superior to the coloured peoples. They laid claim to special rights in their dealings with them. But there are no rights without duties, and their superiority — real or illusionary — imposed on Britons the responsibility of helping the backward peoples to advance. The assumption of this responsibility justified the claim to special rights. This pattern of thought remains important though it is now no longer of general validity. Thus, the obligation to help colonies was accepted without question by nearly all the people interviewed in the course of our attitude survey; 34 per cent considered that we ought to give more help to the colonies than at present, while only 6 per cent favoured a reduction; 71 per cent thought that coloured colonials, because they were British subjects, should receive preference over European foreigners in admission to the home country; 13 per cent did not agree with this suggestion, but their reasons were varied.

Relationships which conform to the old pattern of superiority and responsibility are still often regarded as providing a particularly appropriate setting for dealings with coloured men. In such relationships the Briton thinks he knows what is expected of him, and he feels more at ease. This expectation sometimes underlies arrangements for the entertainment of colonial students. Dr Carey's account of the difficulties some students have experienced over invitations received via the British Council from people who wish to entertain an overseas student is interesting in this respect, although, perhaps inevitably, it is the less successful cases that attract attention. A West Indian student, for instance, related that the first people to whom he received an introduction were anxious about his spiritual welfare and tried to persuade him to attend church with them. The second introduction was to a former member of the Indian Civil Service who spent most of his time explaining how much the Indians had worshipped him, and that by now they must realize that they cannot get along without British guidance, and so on. The third was to some 'left-wing' people who took a great interest in colonial affairs: 'We became quite friendly, but they had a nineteen-year-old daughter and I asked her to come to a dance at my college. To my surprise the whole family became very embarrassed and it was clear that they didn't like the idea at all ... '

Relationships conforming to the generalized pattern of the superiority and responsibility of the Briton towards the colonial were once of a customary and generally accepted character. Colonials received tangible benefits in return for the deference they paid to the white man and the transaction was for a time advantageous to both parties. In Britain the coloured man who played up to British ideas of the 'poor darkie' could do well for himself. Even today, it is said, a coloured bootblack on one street corner will do a better trade than his white counterpart on the opposite side. The converse of this has been that when whites have come into contact with coloureds occupying superior roles they have often been confused and sometimes resentful. Now, however, colonials challenge the patronizing attitude. They do not thank Britons for being concerned about their spiritual welfare. They do not accept invitations of people who enjoy telling how the natives used to worship them. People who invite them to tea but are shocked at the idea of their colonial guests' inviting their daughter to a college dance are apt to be told that they are hypocrites. Rather than be parties to a relationship based on the old norms, coloured colonials now usually prefer to withdraw from it altogether. For a relationship to acquire a customary character it must be acceptable — temporarily at least — to people on both sides. There would be less feeling of uncertainty today about how to behave towards colonials had there not once been a fairly generally accepted pattern which people with colonial and South African associations sometimes try to keep alive.

It is not easy to isolate the positive forces making for the conclusion that no special norms for dealings with coloured men are necessary. One of the more important has doubtless been the reduction of class distinctions in Britain, for once the common people became certain that they were just as good as the nobility so they were likely to decide that coloured people were just as good as themselves. At the same time there has been a reinterpretation of the responsibilities of imperial rule such that the Briton is more conscious of obligations to the individual colonial. Such trends have in recent years been powerfully reinforced by television programmes and the moral condemnation of racial inequalities. This has been to such effect that when some of our respondents referred to 'this colour bar' they meant not racial discrimination but the campaign against it.

The question for an individual of how, in everyday situations, he is to act out his own appraisal of the racial issue is largely answered by the growth of customary practices. Where custom requires that a coloured man be treated in a special fashion the actor must observe the norm or face the likelihood of being punished by his fellows. When the norm endorses equal treatment there is no problem. But when custom is changing the actor has to decide for himself how far he will go in upholding the old norms or in supporting the new ones, and to accept the consequences if he goes too far in either direction. No longer is there any clear guide to conduct; custom has failed him.

It is our thesis that the present position in Britain is one where the customary image of the coloured man and his place in society is changing. In some situations the old, special, norms are still valid. In others the new ones have triumphed. The actor's problem is to decide whether the situation that faces him belongs in the former category or the latter. For example, the question of whether coloured students are to be admitted to university hostels of mixed sexes is one on which opinion is still divided, whereas the acceptability of coloured students in men's hostels is never doubted.[2] Often the general principle is clear, but there are special circumstances which make it difficult to decide. Because of this the Briton is often uncertain how he should behave towards coloured people. This uncertainty is frequently taken as evidence of prejudice when in fact it points to very different conclusions.

95

If the special norms are steadily being discarded, what hinders the pattern of relationships with coloured people from being assimilated to that obtaining among whites? One important reason may be the psychological one that it takes time for people to learn new norms and adjust to changed circumstances. Other influences may also be relevant, but it is our intention here to concentrate upon two of the sociological factors, namely the images of the coloured man as a stranger to British ways and of the coloured man as a stranger in terms of social class. We maintain — and this is perhaps the most important section of our analysis — that in many situations Britons are obliged to treat a relationship with a coloured man as requiring special care and perhaps a different approach (*a*) because he may not understand the norms governing the relationship, and (*b*) because onlookers may regard it unfavourably. The study of the variations from one situation to another can tell us something, not just about race relations but about social life in general.

We gain our knowledge of people by entering into relationship with them, and each relationship can be seen as a sequence of communications between the two parties. The actor interprets the other person's behaviour as having a particular intent and he responds to it so as to indicate his own views or to elicit further information from the other. This interplay between the two of them is built out of words, gestures, tones of voice and of the situation in which it occurs, and results in the two parties determining on particular courses of action or establishing a basis for further and cumulative interaction on another occasion. When the other person refuses to take up the messages that are being conveyed to him the commonest sanction is for the actor to break off the relationship. There is no one norm regulating the entire relationship, but a variety according to which of the parties' social personalities are brought into play. A seller may wish to keep his relations with his customers on strictly commercial terms and to exclude all norms except those relating to the rights and obligations of buyer and seller. His client may seek to introduce other considerations suggesting that theirs is also a friendship and recalling the norms of friendship. He may also draw attention to his personal circumstances, implying that he deserves special treatment and so forth. Social relations are, in Max Gluckman's term, multiplex;[3] every actor is several persons and he is linked to other members of his society through each of his social personalities. To enter into the life of a society it is therefore necessary not only to know the norms of relationship but also to be able to tell which of these norms are relevant. The stranger is not only uncertain of the norms: he cannot read the signals.

A Jamaican woman complained in a broadcast that these signals are sometimes used to convey just the opposite of their ostensible meaning:

> In England, the West Indian has to learn this trick of double-talk. At home we are direct, we say what we are thinking. Here, one has to use words so that a situation — although it exists — is never admitted. For instance, if your hostess asks you to stay a bit longer, even if she insists that you do, you must understand that she expects you to know that her insistence is mere polite form, and that in fact it is incumbent upon you to leave anyway.

How difficult it can sometimes be for the newcomer to learn the unspoken assumptions can be gauged by the story a London landlady recounted:

> The lodgings people sent us an African, though really they shouldn't have done. My husband was against it, but I was sorry for him. We got on well together for about two months, but then he took an English girl in one evening, so of course I had to put my foot down. I don't really blame him, mind, it's the girl's fault as much as the man's and she should have known better. I told him he was allowed visitors, but of course I didn't know he meant white girls.[4]

The Jamaican woman's reactions receive striking confirmation from the words of a Nigerian nurse who had also been exasperated by English reliance upon tacit norms:

> I was warned by friends about English landladies. The English characteristic of a landlady is not saying what she means and so

misleading the lodger into feeling everything is all right until it blows up unexpectedly ... English people are most difficult to deal with even though at most times they appear quite charming. They say 'yes' when they don't mean 'yes'. They are very polite, and this may mean that there are fewer quarrels, but sometimes in life it is a good thing to speak directly. However, since English people speak the same way to each other, I don't think you can accuse them of hypocrisy; evidently they understand each other.[5]

The Briton knows that awkward scenes may develop where people do not share the same customs and cannot take one another's hints; he feels the embarrassing scene acutely and avoids getting into a situation where it might arise. We notice how painful embarrassment can be for members of a tribal society when a blundering anthropologist asks a question which seems sensible to him but indelicate to his hosts, yet we often overlook its significance in our society because we take our own taboos for granted. Most people, at one time or another, will have had the experience of wishing to help someone, but being afraid that if they did so the other person might become too demanding and it would be difficult to shake him off. The occasional case illuminates what must be a general though usually unconscious principle of social behaviour. People fight shy of entering into the sorts of relationship which they feel are likely to get out of control. Their view of how such relationships should be conducted may be unfair to the other party, but it governs their behaviour nevertheless. The Englishman cannot be sure that the coloured man will recognize or accept the former's intention of extending to him only a limited acceptance. He cannot be sure, if he is kind to a coloured immigrant, whether that man will appreciate the limits of his gesture and not take advantage of his kindness. He does not want to be suddenly confronted with an inordinate demand for help, financial or otherwise, which is all too possible when the immigrants have such difficulty in finding work and housing. Consequently, where he suspects that the coloured man may not be familiar with the social norms to which he is accustomed the Briton is inclined to refrain from entering into relations with him.

These considerations suggest that the more a relationship is governed by unspoken norms, and acted out in accordance with signals that are known only to the initiated, the more necessary it is to ensure that the other party is familiar with these conventions. This is frequently the case, but in some relationships the implicit norms are of little importance and it does not matter if the other man is unfamiliar with the culture. Though it is usual to address the bus conductor in a particular manner, to say 'please' and 'thank you', this is not essential. The rights and obligations of conductor and passengers are explicit in the law of the land and if either party infringes them the law provides a remedy. Nor is the landlady greatly worried for herself about taking in a coloured student: she is the landlady, he the boarder — a clearly defined relationship conferring upon her the unquestioned right to give him notice if he offends. The employer is not unduly concerned lest a coloured worker should prove lazy: he can always give him the sack. In each case the actor commands an adequate sanction against an infringement of the norm. But it may not be this that he is apprehensive about. The landlady's power to give a coloured boarder notice is a poor defence if the neighbours object to her admitting him. The employer may be primarily concerned lest an unreliable worker lose him customers or cause trouble amongst his existing staff. We would therefore expect that the weaker the sanctions upon deviant behaviour or undesirable consequences relative to the importance of the relationship to the actor, the more likely will he be to avoid admitting a coloured man to the relationship.

This question of sanctions may well be the key to the second of the paradoxes referred to in the Preface: why should Britons be strongly opposed to any discrimination in the public treatment of coloured people and at the same time be so hesitant about treating them equally in private relations? The coloured man has the same obligation as the ordinary Briton to pay taxes, serve his period of conscription if of the age which makes him liable for this, and to behave as befits a citizen. No one questions that in return he has a right to the same facilities as anyone else; a vote, a seat in the bus, a place in the queue, and the same consideration as one citizen shows another. To hold any other view would be to question all that successive Secretaries of State have said about our colonial 'trusteeship'. On the other hand, people who themselves subscribe wholeheartedly to these principles may prefer not to have anything to do with coloured people in their private lives. This is particularly true of marriage, the most private sphere of all. Not only do many find the idea of themselves marrying coloured people repugnant but they dislike the prospect of any of their relatives or countryfolk doing so either.

In the public sphere there are effective sanctions upon misconduct. The immigrant's rights as a citizen are defined by law: if he steps beyond them he can be punished by law. In the private sphere norms are implicit and sanctions weak. Relations between members of the same family cannot be satisfactorily based on legal requirements, but must stem from common understanding and shared aims. People feel that they have obligations to kinsfolk and relatives by marriage that can be repudiated only in exceptional circumstances. If someone is admitted to the family who does not share their assumptions and cannot play his part in the life of the group, then the family bond may be broken. Hence, the more tightly knit a community the greater is the resistance to intermarriage likely to be. To this it might be objected that the resistance may spring from an instinctive or culturally implanted aversion from intimacy with coloured people; yet this would be too simple an interpretation in view of the evidence that any such aversion is balanced by a powerful attraction towards coloured sexual partners. Whatever the psychological factors it is clear that resistance to intermarriage is an outlook traditionally transmitted and approved, and that social avoidance plays a part in the maintenance of this pattern of behaviour.

The contrast between public and private relationships was brought home to the writer when visiting employers near the Stepney coloured quarter:

During the interviews it was noticeable that some employers were conscious of a conflict between the policies they felt they had to pursue as employers, and those which as citizens they would have

liked to have seen followed. They would set out reasons showing
how it was uneconomic for them to employ coloured labour when
whites were available, but were uncomfortable about the implications of this if all employers were to do the same.[6]

Their roles as employers were geared to private interests and there was
a conflict with their public views as citizens. To the employer, a
coloured workman appears as a risk, for he is unlikely to have the
background of experience that a white worker has and he may need
extra supervision. He is a risk in that if he is taken on other workers
more valuable to the concern may protest. After all, any departure
from the status quo is to some extent a risk. But if all employers draw
the same conclusion a series of private decisions adds up to a public
policy and to one contrary to the country's acknowledged duty to give
all its citizens a fair chance.

The second of our two postulated sociological factors hindering the
assimilation of relations with coloured people to the pattern obtaining
among whites, was that because the coloured man is so extreme a
stranger association with him is something out of the ordinary and is
looked at askance. Unless some explanation is forthcoming the person
who associates with a coloured man may suffer social disapproval or
loss of prestige. Underlying this is the old norm of colonial subordination and the identification of the coloured man with the lower social
classes, to which Dr Little has drawn attention. This identification has
probably weakened of late, especially in university towns, but the
possession of a coloured skin still tends in nearly all situations to mark
a person one or two points lower in the social scale than his other
characteristics would indicate.

A man's status within the local community depends to a considerable extent on the people with whom he associates. If he wants to be
respected he will be careful in his choice of friends, and if there is an
identification of the kind Dr Little suggests, then he will avoid entering
into relationships with coloured people. Little's hypothesis has in fact
been substantiated at several points. The association between dark skin
colour and low-class prestige comes out very clearly from some of Dr

Carey's interviews with London landladies.[7] Two of them made the following comments:

> Taking Negroes is a certain sign that the house is going down. Look at the place next door. Milk bottles left outside, the sheets never changed: a dirty house — no wonder they take blacks.

> Of course, I don't take blacks; I'm sorry for the darkies, that I am, but I know what the neighbours would say: Look at Mrs X, she really has come down in the world.

Though there are other factors than colour, as one Italian pointed out:

> Personally, I don't mind Negroes. Can they help it if they are black? ... Everybody is against them, so they are lonely, they stick together. Take one, before you know where you are the house is full of blacks.

It is not only coloured students who suffer from the ignorance of landladies. One Welsh woman, strongly religious, who was horrified at the idea of taking Negroes, told Dr Carey:

> And I all alone in the house, how could I get help if anything happened? I keep a respectable house, no women visitors, and men to be out by ten. So I don't take foreigners, only Germans, maybe, or Dutch; once a Frenchman came for a room; but no, I says to myself, not with your goings-on!

It is remarkable how many distorted ideas are current about the inhabitants of France; to many people no word conveys a stronger suggestion of 'goings-on' than 'Paris'. If such conceptions of Britain's nearest neighbour are so persistent is it to be wondered at that a few UNESCO pamphlets and a lot of preaching have not greatly affected the popular view of the Negro?

People whose social position is secure relative to those about them will not be so concerned about any unusual associations of theirs being the subject of local tittle-tattle, but social climbers will be very sensitive to such informal sanctions — and very many people are to some degree would-be climbers. Women are, in general, more dependent upon the approval of their neighbours than are men, for, as has been said, 'the man's status is the status of his job, the woman's the status of her home'.[8] The landlady's house is both her job and her home, so she is more exposed than most to the threats of gossip. However, the construction placed upon association with coloured people varies according to the relationship within which it occurs. If a clergyman is seen walking down the street with a coloured man people conclude that they see him performing one of the duties of his office. But if a landlady takes coloured students there is a likelihood of the neighbours concluding that she accepts them only because she cannot get white boarders and that therefore her rooms must be of poor standard. Her role does not fully legitimize the association, though if she were seen walking down the street with one of her coloured boarders there would doubtless be much less occasion for comment than if she were seen walking out with some other coloured man. Association where the white person clearly stands in a superordinate relation to a coloured man evokes no disapproval, but obvious subordination might harm a white man's standing among his fellows.

When a policeman is seen, in uniform, leading a criminal or a prostitute in the direction of the police station his behaviour is interpreted as forming part of the policeman–delinquent relationship and is commended. If he is seen, out of uniform, chatting with a criminal or entertaining a prostitute, his behaviour is interpreted as inconsistent with that expected of a policeman even when off duty, and lays him open to reprimand. In such circumstances onlookers have several indications to guide them in interpreting their observations. But in the case of everyday associations with coloured men there may be few reliable clues, so that contrasting interpretations are often separated by only a hair's breadth. One girl who goes dancing with a coloured student may be seen as having depraved tastes. Another may be thought of as doing a grand job entertaining these poor lads so they won't go home disgruntled — and keeping them away from the Communists!

It is possible that people are more afraid than they need be of the likely effects upon their reputation of being seen with coloured people. But excessive caution in this respect is more easily understood when it is seen how associations which most people would approve can some-times be interpreted in an uncharitable or malicious manner. Fear of what others may think is more likely to weigh with a man in his private life than at his place of work; there, he will be more concerned that the stranger should understand the behaviour expected of him. In some situations only one of the two factors will be important, but in many there will be a mixture of the two.

We would expect the Briton to be more likely to avoid association with coloured men in the neighbourhood where he lives than at his work-place. In the course of his work he may be brought into dealings with the immigrants, but this gives him no cause for concern as his association is legitimized by the work relationship. If the newcomer does not understand the norms of the relationship this need not disturb the Briton, for the sanctions are such that if the coloured man fails to conform to accepted usages he may lose his job. This holds to a lesser extent of relations which are independent of the work process — such as with whom a man sits down in the canteen to eat his lunch, or in informal work arrangements that have not received the approval of the management. While in the district in which the British workers live the structure of relations may be quite radically different. They are not bound to mix with the newcomers, and if they do so they have little defence against either the failure of the immigrants to behave in the expected fashion or the misinterpretation of the relationship by their neighbours. The workers' psychological make-up does not change when they come home from work; their different pattern of conduct is a response to a different social situation.

The observations of research workers and a poll conducted by the British Institute of Public Opinion have substantiated this hypothesis. Commenting upon the results of the poll, Dr Clarence Senior remarks: 'Working relations were regarded [by the immigrants] as considerably better than off-the-job social contacts. Whereas 50 per cent of the out-side relationships were felt to be either "all right" or better, 78 per cent of the workshop contacts were so characterized. There is a four-to-one differential in the "very well, as a friend" category; 10 per cent outside work to 40 per cent at work.'[9] The same conclusion, that 'relationships in the factory are easier than across the apartment landing' has been drawn by other investigators who have either offered no explanation or have not seen it as constituting a problem. We regard this as just the sort of problem which should be meat and drink to the sociologist, for only he has the theoretical equipment to elucidate it.

Earlier in this chapter we maintained that avoidance of coloured people derived principally from two factors: the belief that coloured people may be unfamiliar with British norms and conventions of social intercourse, and the danger that onlookers may interpret association with them to the Briton's discredit. The first proposition was borne out by the experience of coloured people who found British reluctance to 'speak directly' an obstacle to understanding. The second proposition also receives a measure of confirmation from the behaviour of coloured people themselves. With his own acquaintances a coloured man may be known as a doctor, as a student, as someone who has lived in Britain for many years and knows all the Briton's foibles — or he may even be someone born and brought up in this country. But to the man who does not know them each of these is as much a stranger as the latest arrival. It is their colour that is immediately noticed by someone meeting them for the first time, and that brands them strangers. Hence the way some coloured people prefer to keep to the circles in which they are known. Hence, too, the use by others of symbols indicating their social status. Colonial students in London used almost invariably to wear their college scarves or others items of university dress which distinguished them from the stowaway immigrants who, in the post-war years, were often in the news and did much to drag down the social standing of coloured people generally. Former seamen in Manchester who wished to be taken for students might sport scarves to which they were not entitled, and, according to Mr E. B. Ndem, illiterate former stowaways might be seen with copies of *The Times* or *Manchester Guardian* under their arms. In the dockland districts, also, some of the older coloured residents dress carefully in well-cared-for dark suits and take a rolled umbrella on their walks so that they will not be mistaken for newcomers who do not know how to behave themselves.

But perhaps the most effective confirmation comes once again from the Nigerian nurse; she wrote:

> I have never been out with an Englishman. I should find it difficult to explain to my compatriots if I was seen with an Englishman — they might think I had a bad character.[10]

This remark neatly illustrates our contention at the beginning of Chapter III that two different groups may place the opposite construction upon the same physical characters.

The third of our paradoxes referred to the way in which British people's behaviour towards the immigrants can suddenly change in quite a radical fashion when apparently nothing of importance has occurred to alter the situation. For instance, there was a coloured worker who applied for a vacancy in a London firm only to be told that it had been filled. He did not believe this and got his English wife to telephone the firm. She did so. She told them — with remarkable sagacity — that she had a coloured lodger who was a good worker, and asked if they would consider him. They agreed to do this; so the coloured man put on a different suit of clothes, went back, and got the job. Frequently, the slightest recommendation, a reference from an unknown source, or an appealing look, is enough to tip the scales and secure something for one coloured man that would be denied another. Or consider the following extract from a conversation which occurred in a government office in the East End of London; it hints at conflicting feelings of sympathy for strangers in a harsh and alien environment, and guilt over letting down their own side by such sentimentality:

> MR BETTING: Y'know, it's not right these coloured people being given flats in new housing estates when all our people have been waiting so long (*pause*) ... but it isn't easy to see what can be done unless we could find some out-of-the-way spot in the country where they could all be sent.

> MRS SILVER: Hey! What's wrong with the country? Besides, it would be no good sending them there, they'd have no one to batten on!

MR BETTING: (*laughs*) The most inept phrase that's ever been coined is 'to work like a nigger'. They *won't* work. One Friday we had a whole lot of coloured applicants here. The Labour Exchange offered eighty labouring vacancies. They filled five! ... Of course they're happier living in squalor in Golding Street and round there because it's more akin to their own way of living.

MRS SILVER: They'd be afraid of a clean new house.

MR BETTING: They *prefer* to live in such surroundings ... (*after referring to resentment on the part of local white people*) No ordinary working man will work side by side with a coloured man. You can understand it, for these fellows seem to do very well for themselves. They turn up in flashy suits when they're living on a National Assistance allowance. If I was a black so-and-so I'd get an allowance, wouldn't I? ...

MRS SILVER: I have no race prejudice — except the ultimate one.

MR BETTING: None of us have: our experience broadens our outlook. We try to understand the people we have to work with, but the coloured people won't let you understand them. Anyway, we only get the riff-raff here ... Still, if we have no programme for sending them home they ought to be spread out. (*He went on to quote some cases of coloured people behaving very well and concluded*) It's these doss-houses and this filth which causes the problem.

MRS SILVER: (*spoke with admiration of a Negro doctor and of a Pakistani family.*)

MR BETTING: (*sharply*) After all, these people are British subjects — why *should* they have to come into these conditions?

It will be noticed that Mr Betting's final remarks are in direct conflict with those he expressed at the beginning of the conversation.

How are such changes of front to be accounted for? The employer's attitude towards coloured people did not change during the hour or so between the two meetings. What did change was his definition of the situation. People respond not to situations as they really are but as they are thought to be. The employer, we may say, recognized two norms: that he should take no necessary risks when recruiting employees, and that colonials deserve special consideration. At first he knew nothing at all about the applicant and felt the first obligation to avoid risks to be decisive. Later, he defined the situation as one in which the risk counted for less than the obligation to help a deserving colonial. Or the question of imperial responsibility may not have entered at all: the employer may simply have decided that the applicant was as good as any he could expect. In either event the norms did not change, nor the actor's committal to them. The additional information, slight though it was, sufficed for him to define the second situation as being sufficiently different from the first for another course of action to be appropriate. Sometimes, as in the conversation just quoted, an actor's definition changes spontaneously when he reflects upon the inadequacies of his first perspective.[11]

Changes of this kind are not unusual because in the present phase of white–coloured relations conflicting norms of conduct relative to coloured people are so delicately balanced, and because there are few reliable indicators as to how a particular coloured man deserves to be received. Another and amusing example of the first of these factors is provided by Miss Webster when she recounts how a college servant at Oxbridge remarked to a Negro student:

> You know, sir — I always call you sir, don't I now? — Yesterday Bill heard me calling you 'sir' and he said to me 'Oh', he said, 'why do you call *him* sir? I wouldn't call him sir — not a nigger I wouldn't.' I says to him, 'Bill, we're servants of the university, aren't we, and it's our job to serve him as well as the others. It isn't *their* fault that these fellows are coloured. They can't help it.'

For this man the relationship between servant and student was quite explicit in imposing certain obligations upon him, and his conduct was not to be interpreted in any other terms. The role of student elicited from him the same behaviour irrespective of the student's background, and made him unaware how curious his views might sound to some-one who did not consider a dark skin anything to be regretted.

The absence of indicators as to a particular coloured man's merits is another facet of the difficulties of social intercourse with a stranger. Not only is he unable to read our signals but we cannot read his. An employer has various points to guide him when interviewing an applicant for a job — the man's appearance, bearing, previous employment, etc., but these criteria may be useless in the case of a coloured man. Stepney employers seemed sometimes to see the position in very simple terms: some coloured men were good workers, some bad, and the impression an applicant made in the first few moments decided in which category he was thought to belong. A new item of information might lead to an immediate switch-over. Many employers with some experience of the immigrants realize that they are at a disadvantage in this respect. They arrange for a coloured worker who has been with them for a fair time and in whose judgment they place some reliance to see coloured applicants and say what he thinks of them. Men re-commended by existing employees may be shown preference. This obstacle to communication occurs in a variety of face-to-face relations, so that employers often regard a senior coloured man as an unofficial chargehand who can speak to the employer for the others, and for the employer to the others.

Where conflicting norms are so evenly balanced the subordinate party can sometimes manipulate the relationship to his advantage, causing the other to redefine the situation as one calling for benevolence. Africans are usually better at this than West Indians. A Nigerian told the writer how, when he was out of work, he would visit firms in search of a job irrespective of whether they had any advertised vacancies. If they told him that they could not engage him he would not accuse them of being prejudiced, instead he would try to appear as dejected as possible and silently turn to go out; then, he said, 'they feel sorry for the "poor darkie". Sometimes they call you back — they say "no", and then they feel sorry for you.' Men who have been accustomed to subordination are more adept at such ways of winning round their superiors, whereas coloured students and those who most ardently desire political independence are more inclined to stand on their dignity. They have the justification that those who resort to such methods are exploiting and thereby keeping alive the old norms of superordination and responsibility which they would like to see replaced by norms of equality.

Another tactic sometimes employed by the immigrants when matters are going to their disadvantage is to accuse the white person of being actuated by colour prejudice. This can induce him or her to define the situation in a way more favourable to the coloured man. Landladies have recounted how any attempt to reprove some colonial students has drawn accusations of this kind. To prove to them that this was not the case they have at first given way, until they have found that their authority was being undermined.

This view of relations as being so delicately balanced as to respond to slight variations in manner also helps us to understand another superficially puzzling phenomenon. Though so many coloured men complain of a colour bar in Britain there are a minority who quite sincerely say that they have never suffered any discrimination, and who aver that they have nothing to complain about. Sometimes such statements appear to be a psychological defence, for not everyone feels strong enough to admit to himself that he has been rejected when this is indeed the case; but this suspicion is clearly irrelevant to a considerable number of cases. Many coloured people do not demand complete acceptance from Britons: they may have too jealous a love of their own culture or they may quickly come to understand the Briton's viewpoint. Such people get on unusually well with their hosts. Others make demands that are considered unreasonable, so they are snubbed and in their resentment they repeat these demands all the more insistently, until they become incapable of sustaining harmonious relations with a member of the hated white majority. Violent political reactions and acute suspicion of any move on the part of British officials or representatives of voluntary associations have been characteristic of many coloured immigrant groups. Thus the coloured man's approach — cautious or aggressive — easily results in the white man's redefining the situation and acting in a different way — more friendly or less so —

from that which his individual disposition might otherwise have rendered probable.

The more fluid the situation, the greater is the number of possible ways in which it may be defined and the greater is the scope for manipulation. One participant may succeed in getting another to take a different view of the matter in hand, or the general view of the whole community may be changed. Dr Sydney Collins considers that immigrant groups in some towns are more favourably regarded because they have been 'sponsored' by prominent citizens; in effect, their view of how the newcomers should be dealt with has been accepted by other groups and members of the host society and, as a result, material assistance has often been forthcoming. The fluidity in the way Britons define relations with coloured people is also reflected in the results of public opinion polls; responses to questions about the desirability of continued coloured immigration can vary considerably. It was only to be expected that after the 1958 disturbances the polls should show a much higher percentage opposed to unrestricted immigration, for when opinion is fluid widely publicized events can stimulate people to adopt a more definite standpoint. Another factor of importance is that when questioned about something on which they have no set views people are apt to give the reply which they think the questioner wants — or the reply which seems safest. The interviews in our own attitude survey opened with five questions about the colonies and three about contact with coloured people, before the question of immigration was raised. This should have neutralized many of the extraneous influences. The fluidity of opinion and the uncertainty as to the correct course of conduct which underlie the rapid changes in attitude and behaviour make this the sort of issue on which determined leadership from individual Britons can have most effect.

British behaviour towards coloured people is characterized not by aggressiveness but by avoidance of them in relationships which might get out of hand. It is a response not to dark skin colour as a biological fact but to its social significance. If, as we have implied, the meaning of colour is slowly changing in an equalitarian direction as it is realized that the coloured man is not so much a stranger to our ways as was first feared, then such changes should be fairly easily detectable. James and Tenen, at the end of a detailed analysis of how adolescents think of foreigners, reach a conclusion which may be cited as evidence of this. They write: 'It is when colour is disturbing that it is disliked. When it is not disturbing it may be liked or pass unnoticed. It is not disturbing when one feels safe and confident. When one has become accustomed to it, when the coloured person is known and liked.'[12]

When the children discovered that coloured people were much like themselves their uneasiness subsided. Colour no longer had the same significance and they were not disturbed by it.

We may now turn to the last, and in some ways the most problematic, of our four paradoxes. Why should Britons believe their friends and neighbours to be less favourably disposed towards coloured people than they themselves? The facts at issue are not in dispute. For example, in our survey 71 per cent of the subjects replied that they would not mind working with a coloured man, or were positively favourable, whereas only 23 per cent of them believed that other people would not mind. Similar figures were obtained in an earlier investigation, and the responses to other questions bearing upon the distinction between the respondents' own attitudes and their assessment of other people's substantiate the general conclusion.

The kernel of the problem would appear to be the difference between antipathy as a state of mind and avoidance as a feature of behaviour. Army officers are supposed to refrain from discussing religion or politics in the mess because dissension ill accords with comradeship. It does not mean that they are not interested in these topics. Avoidance of coloured people, similarly, is a customary pattern of behaviour and is not to be interpreted as the outcome of the dispositions of the individual members of the nation. The reasons for it are to be sought first in the structure of British social life, which if it is to continue functioning effectively requires that those who participate in it shall understand what is expected of them in particular situations and that others shall be able to rely upon their filling these expectations. There are other factors, however, which lead into deeper waters. For example, not only do Britons regard others as less favourably disposed than themselves but they often seem to regard this imputed reserve as something creditable. Unwillingness to let down the barriers to the participation of coloured people in the more intimate British social activities, unless the new-comers have proved their eligibility beyond question, may be construed as an unwillingness to lower group standards. If groups are to be respected they must to some extent be exclusive. The more exclusive they are, the more membership of them is valued. If a foreigner could obtain complete social acceptance in Britain as easily as he can obtain naturalization papers, then being British would be of much less worth. To retain our pride we must exclude some people at least, and who is more clearly a stranger than a coloured man?

When people say that others of their acquaintance would dislike working with a coloured man, or having one as a neighbour or visitor, they are saying that this would be contrary to the group's norms of conduct, *not* that each one of these people, individually, is unfavourably disposed. This crucial distinction is rarely appreciated. The maintenance of social distance is customary; it is not necessarily actuated by prejudice. It has been maintained that a tendency to consider others unfavourably disposed is in itself a sign of antipathy in the subject — as if he is claiming that others are hostile in order to justify his own antipathy. This argument, while overlooking the point we have been urging, also ignores an earlier finding[13] that people who are very favourably disposed towards strangers are often most conscious of their own remaining antipathy, and thus tend to see more antipathy in other people than these would see in themselves. Others have been apt to conclude that the disapproval of association with coloured people is directed against the immigrants, when in reality it is a sanction applied to the whites who depart from group norms. People may be forced, by the relationships in which they are involved, to observe and even to support customs of which they disapprove, and which a majority of the group may also disapprove of. This is one of the brakes upon social change, but it is also one of the forces that holds a society together.

Part III

THE INTERRACIAL SCENE

CHAPTER VII

STRANGERS IN DOCKLAND

There is no comparison between the amenities of the normal up-town neighbourhood and those of areas surrounding docks. Anything seems to be good enough for the latter, and one is left with the feeling that this may be because the community that inhabits it is too poor to deserve equal consideration with the rest, or because the community is largely seafaring and migrant, and therefore cannot express its demands to the administration.

CAPTAIN F. A. RICHARDSON, R.N., 1935[1]

COLOURED communities grew up in the major ports after the First World War, and as there were very few coloured people resident in other parts of the country Britons tended to identify coloured men with dockland neighbourhoods. The coloured man was assumed to be a seaman, someone who would go back 'home' and for whom no provision need be made. The first coloured men to take jobs ashore and seek to settle down had to contend with considerable hostility from the white population. An African who lived in Manchester told Mr Eyo Bassey Ndem:

> Countryman, you see this country yah, ting dong better lili bit for we black people. When I kam yer in 1912 you no ku ku get no where for sleep. Nah brickyard we kin sleep; no one gree for take we in — nah so we kin waka nah treet so-teh day break. But O yah, ah go tell you this, ee better small pass Liverpool. — (Countryman, you see this country here, things have become a little better for we black folk. When I came here in 1912, we had nowhere to sleep. It was in the brickyard we had to sleep, as no one would agree to take us in. We had to walk the streets until daybreak. But oh! I'll tell you this — it was a little better than Liverpool.)

Another 'Old Timer' told a similar story:

> Things was hard for we people. After that war plenty of coloured people start to come to Manchester. Things better now for you

young ones — you can get good place for stay, you go to dance with white girls — dem days John Bull will shoot you if he see you with him woman. They like their women pass God self.

Between the wars British attitudes towards coloured seamen and residents were unfavourable, but then the white seamen and European inhabitants of dockside streets were not welcome in other parts of the town. Respectable people who lived in the better residential districts wanted nothing to do with drunken seamen and their hangers-on. The construction of docks, canals, railways, and the development of port installations, had cut off the dockland community from other districts. Respectable burghers doubtless found in this nothing to regret. The seaman was regarded as a man apart and different from his fellow-citizens: scores of missionary and charitable bodies sought to save his soul, to reform his ways or protect him from his failings. The isolation of dockland and its inhabitants made both parties less familiar with one another and broadened the social gulf that separated them. This tendency strengthened the identification of the coloured man with those who were conventionally considered the lowest elements in society, and reinforced the image of him as someone strange, who did not belong in the ordinary social world.

The inter-war depression in the shipping industry gave rise to discriminatory practices directed against coloured seamen. Recollection of incidents such as these, at any rate among the older residents, still promotes a deep distrust of the wider society and its intentions towards them. Political sentiment is also important: many coloured immigrants bitterly resent the colonial status of their homelands, and whenever there is racial tension in a dependency, be it Bechuanaland, British Guiana or Kenya, news of events serves to unite the coloured people and remind them that they can never be fully at ease with whites until political equality has been achieved. Discrimination against coloured workers in industry, and cultural differences between them and the host community, such as those of language, religion and literacy — these and other factors serve to keep the white and coloured groups apart. However, a variety of forces have pulled in the opposite direction. The most important way in which the coloured settlers have become linked with the local community has been by intermarriage: white wives and consorts give the immigrants a stake in local affairs which grows with time and the birth of children. Had it not been for such unions coloured seamen would in all probability never have settled ashore permanently. Such is the desire of many immigrants to gain social acceptance and the respect of those who are thought to scorn them, that in spite of the contrary pulls the social gap has tended to become gradually narrower.

The situation in dockland districts has not changed as much in recent years as might have been expected in view of the improvements in welfare services and the reconstruction of blitzed and blighted areas. For many of the more ambitious post-war African, Indian and Pakistani immigrants (but very few of the West Indians), the dockland coloured quarters served as reception areas where they settled first, and then, having got used to the ways of the new country, moved on inland. In Britain the white man is free to avoid the coloured man; if he wishes to have nothing to do with the immigrants he need never do so. But the coloured man is not free to avoid the white man: he is dependent upon him for employment and social esteem. The less a coloured man can master the conventions of British social life the more will he seek to avoid the whites; dockland offers him the best opportunity for a life with other coloured men, free from the continuous pressure of white demands. Thus recent immigrants lacking in the social skills and unable to make their own way in an alien community have inevitably gravitated to the dockland neighbourhoods where they are allowed more licence. From this springs the tension within coloured dockland groups between those who have abandoned the attempt to live up to the standard of the wider society (or, indeed of the societies from which they themselves come) and those who lead as conventionally respectable an existence as they can.

The principal dockland coloured quarters are in Liverpool, Cardiff, Stepney and South Shields. We shall also reckon the Moss Side district of Manchester (as it was in 1945–52) with this group, for although it is far from the sea it shares many of the characteristics of the dockland neighbourhoods.

Relations between whites and coloureds in these districts cannot be characterized by any simple formula. There is no apartheid, but neither is there complete acceptance, and while the immigrants want parity of esteem they nevertheless desire to maintain a group life of their own. It was our impression that in the East End of London coloured immigrants had more contact with whites at their places of work than with their neighbours in the district where they lived. At work white and coloured labourers mix fairly freely, joining in games of cards or football at lunch-time, or 'brewing-up' and sitting round together for tea. In large firms coloured workers are more apt to form a separate group and appropriate particular tables in the canteen, but often friendships spring up between individual workers or a foreman takes a friendly interest in a coloured man. These contacts often lead to an exchange of visits at the parties' homes. Some firms hold annual socials for their staff and, as far as our experience goes, coloured workers who attend with their white wives are generally welcome. The shiftless immigrant is not likely to attend such functions; neither is the migrant worker like the Pakistani, who does not contemplate settling permanently in the country. Contact between coloured workers and their white neighbours may also be limited by circumstantial factors; in the Stepney coloured quarter commercial properties often separated one block of houses from another and the dwellings that had survived the wartime bombardment were sometimes found only in small rows or groups of no more than four or five houses. The local white population included numerous people who had only recently settled there and the rate of residential turnover appeared high. In coloured quarters like that at Butetown, Cardiff, where many of the immigrants have been resident for decades and the local population is relatively stable, there is doubtless much more contact between coloured people and their neighbours.

In a neighbourhood like Stepney most of the coloured men's wives do not come from the district itself and rarely retain strong ties with their own kinsfolk. Thus their lack of family connections tends to exclude the immigrants from some of the emotionally most satisfying spheres of English life. Making friends at the 'pub' or at work can never compensate for this. The institutional life of dockland districts also is often as poverty-stricken as the least-favoured of the inhabitants. Most of the clubs are run by settlements or bodies with missionary intent that cannot identify themselves with the local people enough to supply the missing sense of community.

Mr Ndem, in his Manchester study, pays particular attention to the role of the Church in this respect. He speaks for many other Africans when he recalls how in his home town Sunday meals were cooked on Saturday night; all pitchers in the house had to be filled with water and firewood gathered for Sunday use; the Sunday atmosphere was serene and any form of work apart from the singing of hymns was thought sacrilegious. After this, English conduct and religious practice came as a severe shock. He discovered that ecclesiastical leaders in their efforts to interest the public in Africa had painted a picture of the Africans that was hardly conducive to harmonious relations between members of the two groups. Mr Ndem observes that though church leaders have in many cases tried hard to help immigrants they have rarely been able to win their confidence. The equivocal attitude of many clergymen towards mixed marriages irritates coloured men who see in this issue the touchstone of social equality. Constructive work is easily undone by a single intolerant churchman who is taken as representing all others of his group. The following two cases may be cited from Mr Ndem's study.

A West African:

My father was a strong church man and a lay preacher. I used to follow him to church every Sunday. But since I came to this country I know that the white man only pretends to be a Christian and so I stopped going to church. I'll tell you what happened. In 1947 I went to a church in Liverpool and was told a certain pew belonged to a white man. I said in my country we sit anywhere in the church, so the man said: 'This is not Africa; in any case there is an African Mission here, you can go there.' As from that day I decided not to visit their church. Even here in Manchester when you go to church the whites don't want to sit near you — you feel as if you are suffering from leprosy. No, not me, with the white man's church.

And to balance an Anglican case with a Catholic — an African related how he went to attend High Mass. Before the service commenced a white couple came in and sat behind him. They appeared restive and eventually called the verger; after some discussion the verger came and ordered him to leave his seat as the others were disturbed by his presence.

> I moved to another seat. At the end of the service I reported the incident to the Reverend Father, and he said to me 'you did well to have left the seat, for otherwise we might have lost two souls for the sake of one.' I cannot describe how I felt. That finished me with the Church.

Such cases as these could be multiplied many times over by anyone familiar with the problems of coloured people in Britain.

So far we have attempted to use the expression 'coloured' to cover Africans, West Indians, Pakistanis, Indians and members of some of the smaller immigrant groups who settle with them. Yet 'coloured' denotes a category of people who are a group only in the eyes of the Englishmen. The common treatment meted out to Jamaican and Pakistani alike tends to awaken some fellow-feeling between them, but in background, style of life and objectives they are almost as different from one another as it is possible for immigrants to be.

The Indians and Pakistanis come to Britain to earn a little money and take it back with them to their homeland; very few settle permanently. They do not wish to be assimilated by the majority and they modify their behaviour to suit local conventions only in so far as this helps them to pursue their major objective. The two nationalities seek to defend their own culture — each epitomized in a different religion — from the blandishments of Western ways, and they are not greatly perturbed by racial discrimination. Both Indian and Pakistani immigrants form small communities in the districts where they settle and have relatively little social contact with their white neighbours. Their communities are founded upon common values, customs and aspirations, and enable individual members to live and work without difficulty in an alien country whose language they rarely understand. We may say that they accommodate their social life to the ways of the host country.

It is most unusual for any open friction to develop between Britons and Indian or Pakistani immigrants. The sociological commonplace that friction in a relationship arises from conflicting expectations on the part of those involved is admirably illustrated by a comparison of the two principal groups of coloured immigrants. The Pakistanis demand little of their hosts and are prepared to accept the Britons' definition of the relationship between them. The less trouble there is the more easily will they be able to save money and return to their homeland each with a useful nest-egg. The West Indians, on the other hand, have less definite ideas of returning. Partly this is because they do not see such a sharp difference between the land of their birth and the land of their citizenship; Britain is the 'mother country' and in innumerable little ways they have identified themselves with her from their early school-days. They are British subjects. They are Christians. They wish to be British socially as well as in legal status and they have never imagined that anyone might combat what they have grown up to regard as a praiseworthy intention. They expect to be received as fellow-subjects of the Queen and to enjoy social equality with other British subjects.

News about their countrymen's experiences in Britain has doubtless dispelled the aura round the imperial country's name, but it will take more than one generation before West Indians become as nearly indifferent to racial discrimination as some Indians and Pakistanis. Whether the migrant worker's feeling of 'here this year, gone next' has been spreading amongst West Indian workers we do not know, but at any rate until a few years ago it was true to say that they sought assimilation to the host population. They laid claim to the same rights and obligations as any other citizens and strove to be acknowledged as equals. As a group they were willing to adapt their social life to the conventions of the host country, seeing nothing in their own way of life that needed to be defended against Anglicization. Though they shared certain distinctive customs and aspirations they were not at first fully aware of this, so the bases for community were lacking. Theirs was a group that could attain self-consciousness only in opposition to the whites.

The coloured immigrant, as Dr Landes expressed it, 'guides himself in terms of a logic of complete acceptance, whereas Britons act in terms of a much more limited acceptance'. In their hosts' long-drawn caution the newcomers see rejection. Wounded by occasional but unpredictable experiences of discrimination they draw closer to each other. When their fellows are present they will throw out allegations of racial discrimination of the most exaggerated kind, such that they would not defend in private. These accusations have a symbolic value, reminding coloured men of the need to stand by one another in the face of white exploitation. This apparently negative appeal has played a positive role in awakening national consciousness in various colonial territories, but there the people have a rich background of shared experience. In Britain, Jamaicans, Nigerians and Somalis have little in common that can mark them off as a group apart from their experience of white discrimination. The solidarity of the coloured group has its only foundation in the affirmation of opposition to the white group.

The lack of any true sense of community among West African and West Indian immigrants is demonstrated by the friction that appears in their relations with one another once the stimulus of European pressure is removed. Coloured landlords complain — as one did to us in Stepney — that a coloured tenant will want his room furnished 'down to a needle', and that he will try to take advantage of the landlord's sense of loyalty to the coloured group in order to get more favourable treatment. Coloured tenants say exactly the opposite. From his own experience Mr Ndem agreed with the African who said to him:

White landlords are better than our own people. The white man does not like us, we know, but those of them who give us rooms to live in treat us better than our own landlords. If a coloured landlord knows you are earning a good wage he wants to take half of it from you. So what's all this talk about the white man's wickedness? I tell you, countryman, if the black man has the chance which a white man has, boy! he will make you suffer ten times worse!

In Manchester a number of coloured men have businesses of their own; in 1952 they included a restaurant, two boarding-houses, two small bars, three social clubs, two greengrocers' and a barber's shop. The owners tended, however, to prefer white employees. One of them explained: 'These boys have no sense of time, they still think they are in the tropics where timekeeping is the exception rather than the rule.' When reminded that those employed in local factories were punctual, he replied: 'Yes, they are afraid of the white man.' Coloured workers, on the contrary, alleged that coloured employers were tyrannical, that they paid coloured men less than whites for the same work, and that they showed favour to white employees. A Jamaican who had experienced difficulties with two or three coloured employers told Mr Ndem:

> I paint and decorate, and I swear never to work for a coloured man any more, not as long as I remain in this country. They are worse than the white people, man. Look at that Thomas: I painted his business premises over two months ago and he has not finished paying. Each time I call he will start telling me all sorts of tales about how bad he has been doing lately ... Ah'm going to see him this weekend and if I don't get my money, man, me going to show him up in front of his white customers.

In times of tension between coloureds and whites, associations that represent the coloured group can obtain considerable support from their members, but when tension declines membership falls off and the societies wilt away. Often there is a variety of such associations, each led by people unwilling to accept the leadership of the others, but without real support and readily accused of corruption by the people they seek to lead. Even tribal societies maintained by small numbers of Africans with a common background and a distinctive language often languish unless there is a sense of unity in opposition. Members of the Kru tribe of Liberia, who regard themselves as being very differently placed from their colonial neighbours and in whom this sense of distinctiveness and opposition is most developed, also show the most effective group organization. The same is true of the Somalis from the other side of the continent. Mr Ndem gives an account of the founding of a tribal association in Manchester and the imagery invoked by its convener is indicative of the close association between external opposition and internal unity. The meeting started with prayers, and then in a tense mood the leader recited incantations soliciting the guidance of their ancestors. Then he changed from the tribal tongue to English:

> Gentlemen, I call you say let we meet and join together because John Bull no like we. I bin in dis country going fifty year and see plenty ting. You young peoples must stand together because you know [he rubs his palms, bows in contemplation and utters a name or two of the ancestors] cockroach noh get power nah chicken country.

Cockroaches when found in African houses are eaten up by the chickens, and coloured people, who in Britain are in an analogous plight, can never hope to get power in a chicken country. It was desirable to appeal to this feeling of persecution to encourage the tribal members to form their society.

The form of relationship between one African and another of his own tribe is based upon the sense of mutual obligation. A Nigerian we knew in Stepney was willing to help his fellow-tribesmen by lending them money, but as his experiences had hitherto been discouraging he insisted that they 'made a paper'. Without a receipt he never got his money back. Yet when fellow-tribesmen were asked to put their names to a receipt they felt affronted and went about slandering him because he would not trust one of his fellows. In this situation, as in others discussed above, the norm is recognized by both parties but not accepted as binding in practice because it is not supported by sufficiently powerful sanctions. Thus either party may appeal to the norm in an attempt to outmanœuvre the other. The ideal of the unity of all peoples of Negro descent is only a response to pressure from the whites and it does not effectively regulate relationships between coloured people.

The Indians, Pakistanis and Arabs who settle permanently in Britain attempt to absorb their white wives into their own communities and try to bring up their children to conform to many of the customs of their fathers' countries. The West Africans and West Indians, however, seek admission to their wives' European society, and though they may wish to retain some of their own distinctive customs their relationships with their wives serve to draw them more and more into the white groups. This is particularly the case with immigrants whose children attend local schools. They are anxious that their children shall compete on equal terms with those of their neighbours and accept the aims of the British educational system to an extent that Muslim immigrants never can.

Who are the white wives and why do they marry coloured men? A minority are women who could equally well have married white men but happen to have fallen in love with a coloured man and married him in spite of opposition. The great majority, however, are outcasts from white society — often, though, for no fault for which they can be held responsible. Most have a background of deprivation: they have run away from a home where they were not loved or they have been turned out on account of an illegitimate baby, and the buffetings of misfortune have rendered them personally unstable. Others are psychologically abnormal and unable to live up to the conventions demanded by respectable public opinion. These women may be drawn to coloured men because they are not identified with the society that has rejected them. They may obtain more sympathy from a coloured man than from any other prospective husband, for the coloured man knows that he has little chance of acquiring any more respectable a wife and he does not feel so much the social inferior of a white woman when she is patently incapable of conforming to the standards of her own group. Often the coloured husband gives the woman the affection and security she needs and helps her to rescue an otherwise self-destructive existence.

Some of the women to be met with in the coloured quarters are incapable of any stable relationship with man or woman. They arrive one night from a main-line railway station, perhaps with no personal belongings, spend a few nights with a coloured man and then disappear — probably with some of his possessions. Perhaps the woman has moved on to Southampton; perhaps she is in gaol for shop-lifting. These women were once described to the author by an African as 'the utilities', and we meet them again in Mr Ndem's study. He writes of the woman who, whilst living with a coloured man, goes on the streets.

Sometimes she saves a little of her money against the day when her consort will throw her out; then she will implore him to allow her time to collect her belongings and choosing a moment when he is away will ransack his house, taking his clothes to the pawnshop and decamping with any objects of value. The immigrant then attempts to avenge himself on another woman. When he takes her in he will tell her of her predecessor's behaviour and will keep a stricter eye on her; he may lock his room while he is at work and tell her to sit in a café, or he may even lock her in during his absence. If she goes to work he will insist on her handing over the pay-packet for him to deduct an amount equivalent to her board and keep. Such men are apt to explain that they have been taught a lesson once and that now they are 'smart guys'. If the woman leaves, the man may insist on her collecting her possessions in his presence. Mr Ndem also heard of cases of immigrants seizing some of the women's belongings to make up for their previous losses.

The harsh treatment meted out by some coloured men to their consorts is not always as brutal or unnecessary as it appears. One woman was not unaware of this when she remarked: 'My husband is damn strict. I can't go out without telling him; if I do he will wring my neck. I think it's a good thing, though; some of us want a real good handling.' The observer with a conventional middle-class background cannot help but be surprised by the attitude of many of these women to a 'handling'. Many appear to find life easier if they are given no responsibilities; many derive pleasure from physical punishment. We have documented some cases and incidents illustrative of these and related traits in an earlier work.

The disguises with which people in other orders of society conceal their less acceptable motives and opinions are often absent in dockland. Consequently it is easier to observe there the part played by sexual beliefs and impulses in relations between whites and Negroes. Whites who wish to cast off their inhibitions will often seek out coloured people for company. In such circumstances the factors which ordinarily lead them to avoid association with coloureds are not operative: they are not worried lest the stranger should be unaware of the conventions governing the relationship when it is from convention itself that they seek to escape. The threat of onlookers' disapproval is slight, for whereas a coloured man will be noticed in a white neighbourhood, the white man who goes down to the coloured quarter runs little risk of being seen by his neighbours. This aspect of Negro–white relations was commented upon by James Weldon Johnson, one of the Negro American leaders of a generation ago:

> On occasions, I have been amazed and amused watching white people dancing to a Negro band in a Harlem cabaret; attempting to throw off the crusts and layers of inhibitions laid on by sophisticated civilization; striving to yield to the feel and experience of abandon; seeking to recapture a taste of primitive joy in life and living; trying to work their way back into that jungle which was the original Garden of Eden; in a word, doing their best to pass for coloured.[2]

While a coloured student, describing a visit to a local dance-hall, told Mr Ndem:

> I approached a few girls, bowed politely and asked 'May I have this dance with you?' but met with a firm 'no' each time. Then I noticed that one or two coloured chaps from Moss Side were dancing all the time so I stood aside and watched their method of approach. They just went round, tapped the prospective partner on the shoulder, and said 'Hey, baby, you going to have this dance?' and the girl just followed him. Reluctantly I had to adopt this crude way and I had a number of dances. It seems to me the more refined you appear the less chance you have with these girls.

In London, well-to-do women have been known to support coloured men living in dockland, to visit occasionally a notorious Negro dance-hall, and to invite ill-lettered but powerfully built Negroes from Stepney to Mayfair parties. The more primitive they make themselves out the more are they welcome. We shall not attempt any complete explanation of why coloured men are often sought out for sexual escapades, but will draw attention to two sociological elements relevant to the theory we have expounded. In the first place a stranger will behave in accordance with foreign norms, in a fashion that is the more adventurous because it is implicitly forbidden by the conventions of the host group. But in the second place the coloured man is something more distant than a stranger in situations of this kind. Plagiarizing George Orwell, we may say that he is a non-person. People can throw off their inhibitions with him because he does not know (or they think he does not know) that they are breaking the rules. With a member of his own group an actor would be hindered from certain sorts of behaviour by feelings of shame and guilt; the other's very presence would be an inescapable reminder of what his society expected of him and of the taboos he was breaking. The non-person is someone to whom these rules do not apply; who does not have the same obligations as other people and whom the actor is not bound to treat in the ordinary manner.

The cases instanced by Johnson and Ndem exemplify the image of the coloured man as the exciting stranger. The girls in the dance-hall were perhaps attracted to the novelty of dancing with a Negro in the style of which they are masters. To dance with someone trying to be English — and never quite succeeding — had much less appeal. Examples of the Negro as a non-person are not far to seek — either for English men or women. Two of the first West Indian authors to publish novels about their countrymen in London[3] both tell stories of sexually impotent white men persuading or paying coloured men to have sexual relations with a white woman while they watched. The author heard too many credible stories of a similar character in Stepney's coloured quarter to doubt the occurrence of such practices. Nor is it only whites who may see coloured men as non-persons. Mr Ndem recounts that occasionally two recently arrived illiterate African immigrants would share the sexual ownership of one white woman — a practice unthinkable with an African woman, especially when as in some cases the two immigrants were kinsmen. For a while they did not see the white woman as someone to whom their notions of morality in interpersonal behaviour were applicable.

The tendency to regard members of another group as non-persons, especially in the initial stages of contact, is strengthened by marked differences in outward appearance. A European thinks all coloured men look alike and cannot recognize a particular coloured man until he has got used to their general appearance and can distinguish one from another. Coloured people find the same with whites. The whites' difficulty, referred to in the preceding chapter, of interpreting coloured men's behaviour and appearance is much increased by the tendency to class them as 'all the same' and the strictly perceptual element in this should not be overlooked.

It seems fairly clear that coloured immigrants and white men in Britain regard each other as sexual competitors. Among Englishmen this attitude is almost unvariably unconscious and rarely gathers strength because the number of immigrants is relatively small. Among the coloured men, however, the situation is often explicitly recognized as one of competition. They are well aware that the white women in the coloured quarters are for the most part the rejects of white society, but they appreciate that the women are taking a further risk by casting in their lot with the social untouchables. Some white women who live in these districts salve their pride with the reflection that whatever else they may do at least they do not associate with coloured men. A few are prepared to live with coloured men but are unwilling to marry them. A woman may be shunned by her relatives yet know that they would help her in an emergency; were she to marry a coloured man they might cut her dead. White women who have entered into legal marriage with coloured men have irrevocably broken the implicit white taboo, and their coloured menfolk, who have found how strong that taboo can be, respect them for having been willing to do so. In his dissertation Mr Ndem held that the breaking of this taboo was a significant event, 'for a white woman to marry a coloured man', he wrote, 'implies, in effect, an increase in the coloured population and a diminution of the population of whites'. He continued, 'although these women are the main focus of race antagonism they are, perhaps para-doxically, to coloured men the basis of harmony and the pivot of their social life in Britain'. Coloured men often recount with an air of gratification how on various occasions their white spouses have fought against racial discrimination on the part of other whites. An elderly coloured man told him:

> White women be our god for this country. You see my wife I can't change her for no woman. She stick by me when her her people no want her. You know why some we coloured married to these women? Before this last war if you want work nah your wife will get it for you — you see monkey talk, monkey heary (one monkey understands another); the woman nah him sister so he must give me job otherwise them sister go die of hunger.

Many is the time that coloured immigrants have been heard to say that the friendship of British women has been their salvation.

The Africans' attitudes towards intermarriage reflect their political views. White men in the colonies, they say, form illicit relationships with African women, depriving the local men of potential wives. Later the whites leave these women behind, often unprovided for and with illegitimate children. Therefore, some of them say, they have a right to white mistresses in Britain and are under no obligation to marry them. Others take a more nationalistic view. Running after white women, they affirm, is a sign that their countrymen accept the doctrine of white superiority; the main task is to return home, marry African women and help prove that the coloured man is as good as the white.

White women who have set up house with coloured men often justify their doing so by claiming that they get more romance and excitement from living with a coloured man. 'In Manchester,' says Mr Ndem, 'white women who associate with coloured men are firmly convinced of the potency of coloured men's organs of procreation and the extraordinary satisfaction they can provide.' John Dollard, in his American study, remarks that beliefs about the superior genital adequacy of Negroes are widespread among southern white men; these beliefs serve to buttress social conventions and frighten white women from intimacy with Negroes, while the horrible mutilations and perversions that have occurred at many lynchings lend support to the view that the white men are consumed with jealousy over the assumed superiority of Negroes in this respect. As Dollard emphasizes, this belief is not just a quaint exaggeration but serves an important psychological function. As it is apparently of considerable antiquity, to discover in what countries and at what periods it has been current would be of more than passing interest. In 1795 we find J. F. Blumenbach, who has been called 'the father of anthropology', writing 'it is generally said that the penis in the Negro is very large'. To this he adds a footnote: 'The same was said of the northern Scotch, who do not wear trousers ... I have shown, however, on the weightiest testimony that this assertion is incorrect.' Doubtless the belief is no more true of the Negro than of the kilted Highlander.

In Britain opposition to intermarriage is voiced mainly by the men. They are apt to protest that they feel an instinctive repugnance towards the idea as if it were something unnatural. In truth what they object to is 'their' women marrying the strangers, for the idea of themselves having a coloured sexual partner is regarded as mildly exciting and desirable. There can scarcely be any instinctive aversion from race mixture in view of the extent to which it has occurred throughout history; it is clear that the prospect of intimate relations with a stranger constitutes a temptation for many people. The English proverb 'A black man is a pearl in a fair woman's eye' is no modern innovation, for we find the following passage in Shakespeare's play *The Two Gentlemen of Verona* (1594-5)

> THURIO: ... my face is black.
> PROTEUS: But pearls are fair; and the old saying is,
> Black men are pearls in beauteous ladies' eyes.

In Britain Englishwomen are more favourably disposed towards coloured men than are their husbands, but all writers agree that in the colonies they show far more antipathy than the men do. In both India and Africa white officials mixed happily with the local people until the time came when it was possible for them to bring their wives and families out. The European women's contact with the colonials was restricted, they demanded all their husbands' attentions and disapproved strongly of intermarriage which to them meant the loss of male companions and the possible introduction of foreign competitors into their own community. Sexual jealousy is apparent not only in these comparisons of whole groups, but also in personal relations within British coloured quarters. Just as white and coloured men do not get on well together where women of one group are involved, so there is friction between white and coloured women where men are present. People are curious about members of the stranger group and the sanctions upon intimacy only heighten the feeling of adventure, so that when one person defies convention to marry one of the strangers his or her compatriots may be jealous of their friend who is thought to experience pleasures denied to them.

It is symptomatic of this situation that the question 'How would you like your daughter to marry a coloured man?' is a question posed by men to men. In Britain at least, women can apparently contemplate the prospect more easily. If, in reply to this question men are asked 'What makes you think she would want to?' they are frequently nonplussed, for they do not wish to recognize the possibility of 'their' women being dissatisfied with themselves and their fellow-males of the group – for this is probably what they unconsciously fear.

In discussions of intermarriage several different issues are often confused, and too much emphasis placed on the question of colour. All marriages are mixed marriages, though some are more mixed than others. When they are between partners with a very different background – in national culture, social class or personal experience – the likelihood of their being successful is not very great. It is easy to confuse the general issue (of marriage between West Indians and English girls) and the particular (of marriage between Mr James and Miss Wood). The assumed undesirability of the former is no good guide in an individual case. Neither is it wise for someone to argue from his own personal objection to the general view that it is undesirable for others. Women, as we have remarked, may see the issue differently, like the one signing herself 'Unlucky Wife' who wrote to a newspaper regretting that she had not married her coloured boy friend, who always 'treated her with great respect', but to please her parents married a Lancashire man who 'had not done a stroke of work since'.

Marriage is a topic on which Christian writers have a distinctive viewpoint, though again there is much variation.[4] The Bishop of Dunwich was reported as saying at a meeting in Ipswich that he was opposed to intermarriage between coloured and white races; this did not mean that in no circumstances should it take place, but it should be remembered that in the main coloured races did not approve of whites mixing with them in marriage any more than we did. He thought that intermarriage produced more problems than it solved, and he did not agree that it might be the answer to the colour problem and result in a levelling of the races. 'What you really want', he said, 'is a sane partnership as in a home where the eldest brother has certain responsibilities and the younger element will play their part but never presume to take over from the eldest brother his particular responsibilities to the family.' This is probably a minority view within the Church of England, and the bishop's use of the term 'race' is decidedly unanthropological. On the other hand a Baptist minister has suggested that a marriage between an English girl and 'an eligible, handsome and eminently Christian young man from the West Indies might be more satisfactory than the alternative of marrying an unbeliever or facing involuntary spinsterhood'. A writer who is a member of the Society of Friends has argued similarly: 'the view of the Christian churches is that if two people enter into marriage in a truly Christian spirit, understanding the tremendous moral and spiritual implications of the step they are taking, then differences of race or cultural background will not be important'.

Too little is at present known about the relative influence of unconscious and conscious factors upon British attitudes towards intermarriage for us to be able to set out an adequate explanation of the various forces at work. We can, however, separate several of the elements which play an important part. First, the considerations borne in mind by parents contemplating their daughter's marriage to a coloured man are unlikely to be identical with the views of people for whom the question is purely hypothetical. The parents' first thoughts are likely to be for their daughter: they will fear that she will suffer on account of other people's antipathies and may be apprehensive lest a coloured man will not behave towards her in the manner that is expected in British culture. Secondly, they may expect other people to look down on them because of their daughter's marriage: it may be thought that they have failed to give her the training necessary to make a 'good match', that they must be themselves 'low class' if they have coloured relatives; and that they have let the side down by conniving at intermarriage.

When people are asked their views about intermarriage in general, and are not considering a concrete problem posed by a member of their own family, they are apt to reply that they object to intermarriage 'because of the children'. This response would appear to include elements that are rational, irrational and purely matters of factual information. In the first place we may hold that in view of the emphasis in English culture upon 'breeding true' and upon the importance of a nation's maintaining its cultural identity, it is perfectly natural for people who have been brought up in these ideas to object to something which will produce what they regard as 'mongrels' – offspring who do not conform to the preferred cultural pattern. This is just as rational as the tendency of people educated in a society that glorifies military power to object to provisions for young men to register as conscientious objectors. In the second place, when people object to intermarriage 'because of the children', the observer is often led to suspect that this statement is a rationalization of an unconscious objection deriving from sexual jealousy or similar sources. But how much opposition is due to irrational factors it is impossible to say. In the third place intermarriage is often opposed because people believe that the children of such unions are biologically handicapped. The notion that the children of racially mixed marriages inherit the worse features of both races still lingers, though in truth their genetic endowment is not inferior to that of other children, and may in fact be superior. Similar opinions may also arise from a failure to distinguish between social and biological factors. Mixed-blood populations often are in a precarious position; born in poverty and raised among the disinherited, they are ill-prepared for the difficult role they have to play. Any society that allows future citizens to grow up in squalor, scorned, given only the minimum of social assistance – and that without true charity

— is storing up trouble for itself whatever colour these children are. A society that wishes to abolish social and racial discrimination might welcome an increased number of light-skinned coloured citizens as helping to demonstrate the foolishness of basing social distinctions upon racial characteristics. Whether an increase in the number of such people is desirable or not is a political question, and the answer to it will depend upon whether the society wishes to maintain existing lines of differentiation or to abolish them.

We have moved away from this chapter's initial consideration of racial relations in dockland, but this has been no accident. We have not attempted to describe all aspects of life in these coloured quarters — that has been done more comprehensively in earlier studies — but to select certain features of interest and to explore their significance as indicators of British attitudes and expectations of coloured people.

CHAPTER VIII

RACE AND CLASS AT THE UNIVERSITIES

I couldn't say that I have experienced colour prejudice personally. But there
are lots of West Indians, some of them close friends of mine, who have met
colour prejudice and therefore I feel it could have been me.

WEST INDIAN STUDENT[1]

BEFORE the War there were about five or six hundred colonial
students in Britain. After 1945 the number increased rapidly until
by the beginning of 1955 there were 10,200 colonial students in
the country. More and more parties have been brought to Britain to
study for varying periods in addition to persons conventionally counted
as students: journalists, army officers, pilots, technicians, chiefs studying
local government, and so on. The university towns have become
accustomed to the coloured undergraduate, and people in other
districts are no longer astonished to see a Nigerian walking down the
street in his national dress.

Relationships between colonial students and British people vary from
university to university. In the neighbourhood of the residential
universities a young coloured man is readily accepted as a student. In
the larger industrial towns, and London particularly, a young coloured
man is unlikely to be taken for a student. For all the passer-by knows
he may be a former stowaway or an ordinary worker. Because of the
presence of these other coloured groups the colonial student is identified
with them and is perceived as being in the first place a coloured man
rather than as a student.

Miss Sheila Webster, who has made a careful study of the position in
Oxbridge, says that there the colonial student identifies himself
strongly with his university. His membership of the University is for
him even more important in many situations than questions of colour
or nationality. This applies to other overseas students also: for example,
an Indian who was having a violent dispute with another wrote to

him: 'I have the weakness to believe that, despite your consistent unfairness and gross ungratefulness to me ever since you first met me ... your soul-responses and your sense of honour as an Oxbridge man, a Rhodes scholar and a Tamilian born and bred in the age-old Brahmana tradition, may still be aroused and activized.' As she observes, it is interesting to note the order in which these reference groups are named!

Within Oxbridge the question of social class is of major importance to the ordering of social relationships. This is not to say that class considerations are always present, but that many situations arise in which they are regarded as relevant to conduct. For instance, when two people are competing with one another each becomes aware of factors in his own and the other's background which can be turned to advantage. Usually they are quite unconscious that they are being influenced in this manner. At a residential university of the Oxbridge type where a lot of young people from different backgrounds are brought together in a situation of intellectual and sporting competition, there is inevitably a fair amount of social competition. The more a student seeks to climb the social ladder, the more he or she will be preoccupied with class differences. Miss Webster refers to this, pointing out that students often fail to realize that some of their fellows are Jewish, even though they may have a characteristically Jewish appearance; they become very much alive to it, however, when a Jewish student is more successful than themselves in jostling for social position. She tells a story which illustrates this important point very neatly.

In a women's college there were two women whom she knew to be Jewish: Zoë and Susan. Zoë was always smartly and extravagantly dressed. Her name often appeared in the gossip columns of the university magazine *Chatter*. She had many boy friends, belonging to some of the colleges highest in the Oxbridge hierarchy, and they would drive up to the gate in sports cars. Other men were always trying to meet her and to be seen with her. She led a gay life with groups of young people referred to as the 'fast set' and the 'smart set' that were noted for the consumption of wines and spirits, the ownership of motor cars, attendance at parties, balls and race meetings and frequent mention in *Chatter*. Sought after because of her success, Zoë was very much disliked by many women and some men, and they thought of her as 'typically Jewish'.

Susan came from a German Jewish refugee family and her contact with Jewish culture and religion was probably a great deal closer than Zoë's. She had an olive complexion and Semitic features. She was not, however, socially mobile in the sense that Zoë was; and socially she found her place in a small group of undergraduates and post-graduates who were interested in contemporary psychological and philosophical problems. Miss Webster never heard anyone express distaste for Susan. She was not thought of as 'Jewish' by members of the college, and indeed some women stated quite definitely in casual conversation that there was one Jewish girl in the college — Zoë. Even when she introduced Susan's name immediately following upon this statement the women did not change their opinion. Once when Bridget, a strongly anti-Semitic girl, was expressing her opinion of Zoë, Miss Webster actually asked: 'Do you think Susan is Jewish?' Bridget became bewildered, and said 'Why no. I should never have thought it, at least. She is nice — such a lady.' Miss Webster agreed, and then said, 'I think she is Jewish.' 'Well, she is different,' came the answer. She later invited the two women for coffee together. A few nights afterwards Bridget came to her and said: 'There are two sorts of Jews — the moneyed ones, and the others who are very studious. Elizabeth said she had one-sixteenth Jewish blood in her' (naming a friend of hers who belongs to the same social group and is considered to have a 'good' class background). 'She is very proud of it ... ' Here the conversation was interrupted.

In Oxbridge a coloured skin has the same connotation of an inferior class position as elsewhere, but there are other associations tending to reduce intimacy between white and coloured students. Many of the girls that Miss Webster knew had a strong emotional opposition to the idea of intermarriage. The subject came up for discussion one lunch-time at Sussex Hall among a group of girls who had just been completing a social distance test:

JUNE (to Miss Webster): Niggers have awful hands — it makes me shudder to think of one touching me. If I had to meet one I should try and avoid all physical contact with him. I wouldn't dance with one, and I would try not to shake hands. I think I've got a phobia. Not Indians. Their features are different; their noses are thin, and they haven't those big, thick, flabby mouths. I can't bear to think of a nigger kissing me — and his wide, flat nose.

BRENDA: Don't be silly. They're all the same in the dark.

JUNE: Oh no, they're not. You see, sex is a purely animal thing — just physical — so it matters a lot what the physical characteristics of the man are.

SUE (*who has also filled in a social distance card*): I'm not thinking of the children. I was just considering the physical relationship too, and I couldn't fall in love with one *ever*.

JUNE: I should *like* the children.

INTERVIEWER: Would you rather go to bed with an educated Negro in the University, or a white criminal from the London slums?

JENNIE: Neither. I should commit suicide.

JUNE: The white man. I shouldn't worry about his intellect, because sex isn't a mental thing. You're making me feel quite sick when I think of lying beside a nigger and letting him touch me.

SUE: You're bigoted.

JUNE: I know. And I don't know any — that makes a difference, but that's how I *feel*.

At this point June changed the subject by saying: 'I'd marry a Red Indian though; they're lovely! So handsome!'—and she started singing an American song.

Towards the end of the same meal June said: 'Look at "Trinidad", though' (naming a West Indian girl sitting at the same table who was always called by the name of the island from which she came). 'I'd let my brother marry a black girl, because they are so finely made — better than us.'

The same day the following conversation took place between a different group of women at dinner-time:

TERESA: You know? Negroes have no restraint; I know they haven't. That's why I couldn't marry one. They're so emotional.

INTERVIEWER: Do you know any?

TERESA (*blushing*): Yes, I meet them in Oxbridge. Of course, they're better at art than we are — musical, good at acting and singing — and sport too. That shows that they're more emotional and have a capacity for expressing it.

BIDDY (*who said she would marry one if she loved him*): They co-ordinate better, don't they? But why didn't you put in Jews? (*i.e. on the social distance form*). I could pick a Jew out anywhere.

TERESA: Yes, as a race they ought to be put in too. I couldn't marry a Jew.

BIDDY (*who has lived in Germany, where her father was with the occupying forces*): We're more like Germans than Jews.

TERESA: Marrying a Jew would be very much like marrying a black man. Just as different.

CHRISTINE: I couldn't marry a Chinese either; they are so oily. And yellow skin — horrible skin! I don't like their black hair ...

BIDDY: Oh, Chinese are rather sweet.

INTERVIEWER: Which would you rather marry — a white man from the slums of London, or an educated Negro?

BIDDY: The Negro, I think.

TERESA: Oh, how *could* you! I'd marry the white man.

CHRISTINE: Yes; you see, you would share certain inherent things in the British character — something deep and traditional — inbred in us. Certain values. You see, the foreigner wouldn't like cricket or living in a foggy country the same.

Fourteen out of a hundred Oxbridge girls filling in a social distance card indicated that they would be willing to marry an African. Many of those who said they were unwilling to do so justified their views by reference to 'the misery of half-caste babies', to Africans' 'lack of intelligence' or to the undesirability of 'mongrelization'. Very often they referred to the social situation of interracial marriages, as when one girl said:

> I suppose I should marry them all in theory, but not in practice. I *couldn't* marry an African. Not because of my own feelings, but it is so hard on the children. I wouldn't let my brother marry an African either. I think that, if I thought about it, I shouldn't marry any of them in practice. I don't know any of them except Indians.

A medical student was very concerned to explain her attitude, and said:

> I admit there is no logic in it, but I just *feel* that intermarriage is wrong. They have different-sized heads, don't they? So their brains must be different. Their genes are different too. And it is awful for the children; they have no roots in either culture; they don't belong anywhere. Would you like the whole world to turn khaki? I don't really believe in marrying foreigners at all — cultural differences are too great.

A final example expresses the conflict felt between morality and emotion:

> This is fearfully frank. On principle I would accept members of all these groups into anything as persons, and not as belonging to certain races, but I *couldn't* marry a coloured person — although every ethic would tell me to.

In most cases of objection to intimacy with a coloured man no explicit reason is given; where responses are offered, as in statements such as that a coloured man would not appreciate cricket(!) or would be too emotional, it would clearly be foolish to take them at face value. Objections on aesthetic grounds ('awful hands ... wide flat nose') ring more sincere and deserve careful consideration. Individuals grow up in our culture to regard certain kinds of features as beautiful, others as ugly. Red Indians are romanticized, Negroes regarded as having an appearance the opposite of the ideal. In a romantic age people identify themselves strongly with heroes and heroines of screen and story-book. To find oneself paired with the villain instead of with the star destroys one's image of oneself, which may explain why women's objections to marrying coloured men frequently appear to be stronger than their objections to intimacy with them. When someone is literally afraid of any contact, then the observer is inclined to suspect that the fear springs from unconscious identifications of coloured features with repressions, desires or unacknowledged fears. But though factors of this kind are involved in some cases it does not follow that they offer an explanation of the milder forms of repugnance. The interdependence of the image of the self and the image of the stranger may be a factor equally deserving further examination. It is also important to consider why this repugnance is usually professed by white women of Negro males, scarcely ever by white men of Negro women, and rarely by anyone about people of the other group of his or her own sex. From this variation it would appear that in the vast majority of cases revulsion is culturally conditioned. In a few instances it may be due to purely individual factors, but in the great remainder it is a reflection of the pattern of social groupings (sexual and national in particular) and the significance attached to features indicative of group alignment.

In a university town like Oxford or Cambridge emotions of this kind are not so likely to be crudely expressed. Standards of courtesy are relatively well defined and the student's role is clear. There are also a number of people who seek out colonial students in order to befriend or help them. These people often act as if they consider they are doing the colonial student a favour, and Miss Webster likens their behaviour to that of the local aristocrat who initiates a conversation with a villager, graciously showing interest in the inferior person; but all the time each knows that the superior person can direct the conversation in any way he pleases, can ask all the questions and answer none, and can terminate the meeting when he wishes. This, she says, is a 'conditional philanthropy' in that it is dependent upon the acceptance, on the part of the colonial student, of an inferior status. The sort of thing that happens is that, let us say, Allasani, sometime after his arrival receives a note from a Mr Greenwood inviting him for coffee one evening. Allasani has never met Mr Greenwood; the note looks all right and it certainly is very kind of him; only, what does he want to get out of him? Allasani asks himself. Is he just curious about coloured students? May he be retired from the colonial service and be nostalgic about Nigeria, or whatever country Allasani comes from? Or is it religion that he is going to be dragged into? With these suspicions in his mind Allasani attends the coffee party, and sees that the three or four other students invited are also coloured. Immediately he begins to feel a bit uncomfortable; he is *it* again; he is put into a category — that of people with coloured skins. Mr Greenwood talks about an organization to which he belongs, which he says is very interested in the welfare of coloured students; he hands them a few pamphlets and tries to get them to talk, but the conversation is not flowing very easily. He tells them about the aims of his organization, which he suggests they may want to join. Usually Allasani comes away feeling a little depressed after this kind of party, hoping he can avoid the man if he meets him in the street, and determined that he will never join this organization. Mr Greenwood, on the other hand, is left feeling that the coloured students seemed very ungrateful, and when his next invitation is left unanswered he may begin to think that these fellows are not worth bothering about after all.

One West Indian remarked: 'You know, in college they invite you to a party so as to have it a bit unusual, and they think they are doing you a favour. When you get there there is someone who plays the flute and someone who stands on his head, and a coloured man.'

Another said that he was always put on his guard in a conversation which began with the embarrassed question 'Excuse me, but where do you come from?' as 'if there were something slightly indecent or rather humiliating in the subject'. As Miss Webster concludes, 'it would seem that the Negro would willingly pray with Florence Nightingale, "From philanthropy ... and all the deceits of the Devil, good Lord deliver us".'

In Oxbridge the coloured students' societies are mostly social clubs of much the same kind as other student societies, and arrange similar activities. These clubs serve to socialize the newcomer, to teach him his role in Oxbridge and the various patterns of behaviour expected of him. The leaders of such clubs are both mediators and models. They check behaviour which is considered unsuitable, encourage that which is socially approved, and accept the existing system of relationships. They attend the tea parties and are willing to tolerate a certain amount of patronage as a regrettable but perhaps understandable feature of the general situation. The London students are much less tolerant, for they get less chance to meet educated whites on friendly terms; they object bitterly to anything savouring of patronage, for this they perceive as a weapon used against them, and as a form of behaviour expressing a philosophy that they oppose root and branch. In London a much less clear role is offered to the coloured student, and a much less favoured one. This role the student rejects. He bands together with his fellows not to practise British customs, but to keep alive memories of his own culture and to protest against the treatment he receives from the white majority. The more successful Negro student societies in London have been of a political character. Their leaders have not, as in Oxbridge, presided over social gatherings; they have been leaders of colonial protest.

This difference is well brought out by a story told by Miss Webster of a coloured student who came to Oxbridge to undertake advanced studies. As an undergraduate in London he had played an active part in organizing opposition to a Government proposal and the publicity he attracted had given him considerable prestige amongst his fellow-countrymen. All the Africans had heard of him and knew of his ability as a group spokesman in situations of conflict. Yet after meeting him several of them expressed doubt as to his ability to become a leader at Oxbridge, for he could not adjust to the new situation he had entered; he wanted to be back in London where racial hostility was approved by his fellow-countrymen and where he did not have to learn new ways of behaving, or observe the irritating social usages customary among members of the English middle classes. The coloured men who were involved in meetings between him and white undergraduates sometimes apologized for his behaviour, and he himself explained that he was 'embittered' by his experiences. He tried to carry over into the Oxbridge situation behaviour learned in the situation of race relations at London; for example, when nominated as a member of one society he announced that he would not join unless another member, the son of a white East African settler, left it first. After a time, although retaining formal membership in some associations, he retired from social life within the University.

In London the colonial student is more exposed to the rough edge of British attitudes and comes more readily to identify himself with coloured people as a whole. In a survey carried out by P.E.P., students were asked if they themselves had any personal experience of colour prejudice, and if so in what form. Of the Africans, nearly three-quarters of the total number in London and in the provinces stated that they had had such experience; one-half of the West Indians, and one-quarter of the Asian and Mediterranean students replied similarly. Of those in London, over half of the Africans had found colour prejudice in looking for accommodation, but in the provinces the proportion was smaller. The contrast was still greater for the West Indians and the students from the remaining territories; over half had experienced colour prejudice in London, only about one-tenth had done so in the provinces. It should, however, be emphasized that resentment of white attitudes may be strong among coloured people who have no personal experience of discrimination. They identify themselves strongly with their fellows, and when one individual has an unfortunate encounter many of his friends may be just as irate as the man who had suffered, for they feel that if it could happen to him it could equally well have happened to them.

It is not easy to detect any very definite pattern in the situations in which colonial students find themselves most subject to discrimination. From the P.E.P. data it would appear that both extremes of isolation and congregation are unfavourable. They report that students in the provinces and relatively isolated areas showed a greater degree of sensitiveness to the colour question than larger student bodies in bigger centres. But in London many students have little contact with Englishmen or English life; they gather in regional student associations with fellows from their own country and miss one of the chief benefits of studying overseas. Some students react violently against their reception; others are of more flexible disposition and better able to see their discomforts in perspective. The P.E.P. writers say that 'a surprising number of colonial students — not infrequently those who have been in Britain for a number of years — did in fact say that their compatriots, and they themselves, were over-hasty to seize upon colour prejudice as an explanation of conduct'. One student whom the writer knew personally said that he had found British administrators in West Africa so arrogant that he came to this country with a strong antipathy towards the people. Four years in friendly contact with other students and lecturers in London sent him back strongly pro-British. A Kenya student told the P.E.P. interviewer: 'I have no experience of colour prejudice myself and I take the view that United Kingdom people keep away from people whom they do not know unless introduced; it is not always a question of colour.' A student from Uganda said that he neither expected nor found colour prejudice in Britain. A young man of mixed race from British Guiana considered that 'my colour makes things more difficult, but white foreigners are faced with many of the same problems as those with which coloured students have to contend'.

Colonial students find the difficulty of getting suitable accommodation their biggest problem. Many of them prefer to live in hostels where they usually find the facilities better and the atmosphere more friendly. As a Nigerian wrote: 'The British Council has certain pet theories they want to put in operation, like the idea of doing away with hostels and placing all students in families. I think this policy wrong because the largest number of English families who take in colonial students do it because they need the money badly and not really because they are interested in them personally; and only a small number of families take in colonial students because of a genuine desire to help them.' Overseas students also express disappointment with other aspects of British life. Many mention their disappointment about religion. A Nigerian said: 'I was educated at a missionary school, and the people there had given me the idea that England was a Christian country. But apart from the Student Christian Movement, nobody that I met seemed at all interested. It seems that Christianity is an article for export only, to keep us quiet.' They complain with vehemence also about the average Englishman's ignorance of life in the colonies. Another Nigerian wrote: 'School-children should not be brought up to think that we live in trees, that we are savages, and that we are inferior beings little higher than animals. Many of the comic books which these children read should be revised so as to exclude anything portraying Africans as inferior beings.' Worse still, however, is the Englishman's indifference. As a Jamaican student justly observed: 'I think that being a fellow-member of the Empire means nothing to the average Englishman because he knows little about it and cares even less.' Students point out that Britain is still politically responsible for vital decisions affecting the colonies and that the electorate is ill-equipped to judge such issues. They think that an improved understanding of colonial peoples and the problems that face them in moving to independence would do more than anything else to improve relations.

The political factor is also of the greatest importance. Dr Carey holds that the extent to which awareness of colonial status affects West Africans' interpretation of their English experiences can scarcely be emphasized too much. The point is strikingly illustrated by his comparison between students from British West Africa and those from the independent state of Liberia. One Liberian student remarked: 'People respect us because we come from an independent country, and they know it. Some students from British West Africa see prejudice in everything they experience. I myself think that if you behave well, and don't expect any special favours, people will treat you O.K.' On the same grounds one might expect an improvement in relations as colonies become independent. It is generally agreed that this has happened in the case of the Indians and Pakistanis: the burden of resentment has been lifted from the former colonial and the Englishman no longer feels that he is in some way responsible for him. The same is to be detected with West African students who, as their country's independence has been assured, have gradually lost interest in attacking the British and turned their thoughts to the new problems facing their own countries. Nevertheless, in the years round about 1949-53 there was a bitterness and suspicion among many groups of colonial students that had to be personally experienced to be believed. A preliminary report of colonial students' views published by P.E.P. attracted considerable interest; it did not adequately portray the vehemence of some of the more politically minded students but its critical tone (which appeared quite mild to people acquainted with the position) was a source of astonishment to many readers.

A number of students stay on in Britain after qualifying and practise in some profession. In many instances such people become the leaders of the coloured communities in their districts, for though their occupational status brings them favoured treatment this is not always known and in public places they are liable to receive the same slights as the newly arrived immigrant worker. Neither can it be said that within their own professions the colour of their skins is of no significance. Many cases have come to light of apparent racial discrimination within the medical profession. One doctor, for example, carried out a small experiment. He applied for all the suitable medical posts advertised in a particular periodical. In every second application he stated that he was coloured, but made no mention of this in the others. To each application that included reference to his colour he received a reply regretting that the post had been filled. In response to all the other applications his name was placed on the short list of eligible candidates. As he had a large and flourishing practice of his own he had no intention of accepting any of the posts had they been offered him.

Coloured professional men, doctors, university teachers, writers, clergymen, etc., and popular entertainers and athletes, may be said to constitute the coloured social elite in Britain. They are already a fairly distinct group but they often seek to emphasize further the factors that mark them off from the mass of colonials. Their position has been the subject of a short but intensive study by Miss Violaine Junod. She found appreciable differences in the pattern of relationships between them and the English public. The professional men have to contend with resentment and continuous opposition from white colleagues who perceive them as competitors. They show themselves of comparable intellectual stature and disprove the myth of white superiority, and the white man, Miss Junod says, finds it hard to accept this. On the other hand, physical ability on the athletics track or an exotic artistic talent is still compatible with notions of 'magnificent savages' and 'different mentality'. A coloured artist is not a continuous threat to his white colleagues; his popularity is as dependent upon the fans' whims and fancies as is theirs and his speciality is often distinctively Negro, such as the singing of calypsos. These may well be crucial factors, though it is probable that Miss Junod misinterprets the 'myth of white supremacy', as a principle of white behaviour. Earlier it has been suggested that English people are unaccustomed to meeting coloured people in relationships where the latter have the advantage, and they resist this as socially inappropriate. In the case of the entertainer, however, it is the public that has power over the artist and can make or break his reputation. The public is willing to shower favours on the individual coloured man so long as it is clear who is calling the tune.

The social elite, according to Miss Junod, provides the coloured minority with two different kinds of leader: the compromise leader and the protest leader. The first is an intermediary between the two racial groups who confines his activities largely to social representation, and in particular to representation upon the many bodies which have sprung up in recent years to express opinion on colonial affairs. There is a feeling, writes Miss Junod, that 'something must be done' about the demands of the colonial people and that their causes should be espoused by sympathetic whites. In each case such organizations invite a prominent coloured personality to sit on their Executive. Those invited are normally non-political figures whose names are not associated with any party or colonial nationalist movement. Their role on these bodies can easily be seen, we are told, as that of a figure-head — a large human poster advertising to the public 'no colour bar practised here'. Their participation is nominal; they in no way direct policy-making and in fact few attend meetings with any regularity. They recognize the role that has been offered them and avoid embarrassment by acting in the way expected of them. There is also a tendency for organizations holding a public meeting dealing with colonial issues to get at least one coloured speaker on the platform. The protest leader, however, usually gets little or no recognition from the whites; they regard him as an irresponsible agitator, an impossible person to work with. The protest leader maintains close links with colonial political movements and is often their adviser. He refuses to accept the present system of relationships between whites and coloureds, but denounces white oppression, reserving a special venom for the Colonial Office and all its works. Though the protest leader often by his inflexible attitude of defiance earns the dislike even of whites sympathetic to his cause, he earns the respect and esteem of the majority of coloureds; they regard him as their true representative, not the compromise leader who is only 'acting white'.

In 1952 when Miss Junod inquired into the work of the various bodies in London concerned with colonial affairs and the welfare of colonial students, she was struck 'by the gigantic proportions the "communist bogy" has assumed in British circles, both official and unofficial. People to whom I spoke, organizations with whom I worked, seemed to lose all perspective and objectivity on this issue. Communism had come to be confused with, and to stand for, all sorts of things, most of them in no way connected with the communism of the textbooks or the communism of present-day Russia. Some of the things people associated with communism included: the demand of colonial peoples for self-government; the demand in West Africa for the Africanization of the civil service; the colonials' wish to have more say in the running of their affairs; their demand for social equality; the desire of some coloureds to take out white girls; their adaptation to Western ways of life; the opposition to Central African Federation … etc. Even if, perhaps, this was not strictly communism, then, so they said, communism was to be blamed for it.' 'On closer analysis', she writes, 'the various organizations are all more concerned with combating the spread of communism among colonials than with presenting colonial issues. Each has a different recipe: some believe that it can only be defeated by publicly denying any association with communism; others by drawing Communists or fellow-travellers into their fold and weaning them away.'

Attending the meetings of these bodies Miss Junod sometimes found what she termed the 'zoo situation'. 'I could not help feeling, when attending formal receptions, that the coloureds invited were "on show". Whites spoke to them amiably, sat with them, but seemed to regard them as objects of interest rather than as people. Let us refer to a particular incident. The "objects of interest" were on this occasion visiting Emirs from Northern Nigeria, accompanied by their retinue: manservants and interpreters. Their apparel, so vividly different from ours, drew approbation from all: magnificently embroidered robes, encrusted with gold and of the most exotic colours, turbans and headdresses towering over finely drawn ebony faces. The whole group impressed me with its aura of dignity and presence. As they entered, I was conversing with an English lady; her first comment was, "Aren't they sweet!" followed, as they sat in a semicircle of chairs and were offered tea, by "Now they're happy." And the semicircle of chairs was placed opposite them for the onlookers. I gradually extricated myself from my lady, who, having heard of my South African nationality, had explained: "Of course, now I understand your interest in West Africa: they've all got the same mentality." I moved to join the onlookers; three white women who gazed as if they were strange and curious animals. Conversation was very stilted and formal: Did they like English food?, where did they come from?, etc.'

Those organizations which are politically more left-wing are primarily concerned with colonial issues and invite the public support of leading coloured figures provided they are not regarded as being too political. The more right-wing organizations are much less interested in changes in the colonies; they devote more attention to the welfare of coloured students in Britain and by this more personal approach complement the activities of the former. There is also a variety of official and semi-official services for student welfare. These latter organizations, however, do not as a rule seek the help of resident coloured leaders. The students must, so far as is possible, be guarded from agitators and irresponsibles; it is thought best that they should be introduced to British life by whites who can keep a fatherly eye upon them.

In one respect Miss Junod's report fully reinforces Miss Webster's observations. Members of the coloured elite resent nothing so much as patronage; it epitomizes all the old norms as to the coloureds' subordinate status. One of them told her 'a West African friend of mine at the University was a happy and popular member of the Student Christian Movement, but the suspicion that people might feel forced by their Christian principles to be nice appalled me and I never joined it ... I could not bear the thought of being patronized, or being the object of someone's Christian charity.' Miss Junod was impressed by the number of occasions she heard such remarks as 'Isn't he good, *for an African?*', 'it's amazing, considering he's coloured', 'Doesn't he speak English well, for a Negro?' This led her to conclude that the coloured social elite suffers far more from patronage than from discrimination. Patronage is galling because it makes the person towards whom it is directed feel that he or she is being used as an object and is not recognized as an independent individual. The point has been well made by Jean-Paul Sartre. He has described how, during the occupation of France, the Nazis made Jews wear yellow stars to show who they were.[2] This in turn led some French people to greet the Jews they met with extra courtesy, so as to show their sympathy. But the Jews found these demonstrations very distressing. They felt they were being treated as objects that provided the liberal and virtuous with the opportunity of making a generous gesture. The liberally minded Frenchman was entirely free, on meeting a Jew, either to shake him by the hand or to spit in his face, but the Jew had no choice in the matter; in Sartre's words, he was not free to be a Jew.

In a later essay Sartre states that this argument does not apply in the case of the coloured man.[3] The Jew shares a common culture with the European and is not always recognizably Jewish: 'the Jew, a white man among white men, can deny that he is a Jew, can declare himself a man among men. The Negro cannot deny that he is a Negro, nor appeal to the abstract notion of one colourless humanity: he is black. Thus he is driven into authenticity.' However, this qualification seems to have been inspired by political wishful thinking rather than by observation, for 'unauthentic' coloured men have been a common feature of the interracial scene. Indeed, it may be held that the structure of relations between blacks and whites has on many occasions been such as to encourage the multiplication of 'Uncle Toms' and 'white man's niggers'. In the days of British colonization in West Africa literate Africans were encouraged to become as European as possible but yet were never fully accepted; they, at least, were driven into *un*authenticity. This phase has now passed and the Uncle Toms have given way to the leaders of colonial protest, but traces of the earlier attitude towards European civilization survive.

Miss Webster cites an extreme case of a West Indian student who had failed to make a true assessment of his situation and to face up to it in the manner Sartre calls authentic. Mr Stephen was a post-graduate student at 'Mylbridge' — a pseudonym for one of the colleges highest in the Oxbridge social hierarchy. The following conversation is recorded:

INTERVIEWER: You are reading physics?

MR STEPHEN: Yes; not in order to become a physicist, but so that I may be able to use scientific concepts in philosophy. I am not interested in physics as such, but in the relationship between science and recent philosophical thought.

INTERVIEWER: Whose lectures are you going to?

MR STEPHEN: Oh, some philosophical ones. I like T——, only he takes a long time getting to the point. The lectures here are much slower and more dreary than they are at London. They spend a whole lecture talking about a qualifying clause.   •

INTERVIEWER: Have you met any interesting people?

MR STEPHEN (*is silent. Then says*): Oh, several philosophers, you know. Mylbridge is composed of a great many post-graduate research people, as I am. The physics students are not a bit interesting.

INTERVIEWER: And women?

MR STEPHEN: I haven't noticed. I am too busy.

INTERVIEWER: I believe there are some other West Indians at Mylbridge.

155

MR STEPHEN: Yes, I think so. At least, I have seen some men who look like West Indians, but I haven't bothered. I am not interested.

INTERVIEWER: Have you met any other West Indians in the University?

MR STEPHEN: I came across one, but I can't remember his name. He invited me to the West Indian Club, but I didn't go. I haven't time to mess around with that. I have joined the Philosophical Society.

INTERVIEWER: Are you going to join any of the religious societies?

MR STEPHEN: Well ... I am interested in the relation of science and religion. I have more in common with Socrates, really.

Sartre's remarks about relations between Jews and Gentiles in war-time France apply quite closely to the situation of coloured people in Britain. The same tendency to use coloured men as objects providing the virtuous with an opportunity to demonstrate their feelings is apparent in some of the incidents and opinions quoted earlier. It is shown, for instance, in the case of the Worcestershire bride who asked an African curate to officiate at her wedding in order to show that she did not approve of colour prejudice. The coloured man in Britain can never be sure whether the people whom he meets will use his acquaintance as a means of displaying their sympathy or their hostility, or whether they will approach him as one man to another. Nor is the African always free to be an African, for he finds that whites often behave towards him on the assumption that he is a simple savage, or on the equally irritating assumption that he accepts the Englishman's views of what is desirable. African culture is ignored or is not recognized as legitimate. The Englishman often has difficulty in accustoming himself to the idea that the African may have his own outlook or may not accept the European's criteria of judgment. This obstacle to understanding is felt most acutely by the more educated coloured people, whether they are students at the universities or have joined the elite of coloured professional men, but it is characteristic of the whole situation of racial relations in Britain.

CHAPTER IX

COLOURED WORKERS IN INDUSTRIAL CITIES

I have been surprised at the way our people have adopted these coloured
chaps. Before the coloured staff started work with the department, I thought
the whole thing was a big mistake. I thought they would not be able to do
the job. I have been proved wrong.

TRADE UNION LEADER OF BIRMINGHAM BUSMEN, 1954[1]

THE post-war migration of West Indian workers to Britain may be
said to have begun in June 1948 when S.S. *Empire Windrush*
docked at Tilbury with 492 would-be settlers on board – all
males save for a single girl stowaway. During the next three years the
number of migrants remained about 500–700 per annum. From 1951
to 1953 the volume fluctuated between 1750 and 2200, but after this
more ships became available to transport migrants and the numbers
shot up as fast as the green pawpaw tree: 10,000 in 1954; 24,500 in
1955; 26,400 in 1956. Since then numbers have fallen off: 22,500 in
1957; 16,500 in 1958. The countries from which they came are given
in the adjoining table.

The proportion of female and child migrants to adult males increased
steadily as the first groups settled in and the idea of migrating began to
appeal to wider sections of the West Indian population. Thus in 1955,
7000 of the newcomers were women and 300 were children; in 1956
there were 9000 women and 870 children; in 1957, 9400 women and
870 children; in 1958, 7770 women and 1080 child immigrants.[2]

Owing to the difficulty of separating coloured immigrants from
colonial-born whites in the census tables it is not possible to give any
accurate figures of the total coloured colonial and commonwealth
population of Britain. Estimates of the size of the Indian and Pakistani
groups are particularly liable to error as many of the latter have been
counted as Indians.

The principal coloured communities, students apart, have been the

African, Arab and Pakistani groups in port areas; Indians, Pakistanis and West Indians in London and the Birmingham region; and smaller West Indian groups in all the main industrial centres: Manchester, Nottingham, Leeds, Sheffield, Liverpool, Wolverhampton, Bristol, Ipswich, Coventry, etc. The West Indian migrants, being more familiar with English ways, have been more adventurous in spreading out wherever employment was offered.

TABLE III

Sources of West Indian Immigration, 1955-6

Country of Origin	1955	1956	1957	1958
Jamaica	17,900	15,200	13,800	10,100
British Guiana	400	1200	250	500
Barbados★	2000	2000	2100	1100
Trinidad	800	1400	1300	900
Windward Islands	1300	1600	3100	2100
Leeward Islands	2000	2400	2000	1700

* Excluding migrants forming part of government-sponsored schemes.

The employment pattern of Indians and Pakistanis is quite different from that of West Indians. The former are for the most part ignorant of the language, frequently illiterate, often of slight physique, and willing to take work of a kind shunned by other men. Their chief concern is to earn as much as possible to take with them back to their homeland, and to this end they will take on as much overtime work as they can. Because of language difficulties they are often employed in large groups with a leader who serves as interpreter and helps the newcomers. Some Indians and Pakistanis take the opportunity to acquire skills that may be of value to them later, but the majority prefer to keep to fairly simple work. Their regularity of attendance and low rates of turnover in firms where arrangements are suited to them has earned them an excellent reputation in districts where workers have otherwise been hard to recruit and retain. 'Frankly,' said the personnel manager of a large car factory in Coventry, 'we should be completely lost without our coloured workers. Our foundry just would not keep going.' At the factory there were a hundred coloured workers, working at the furnaces on material-handling and track-feeding. 'They don't mind how hard they work, but they seem to prefer that kind of job,' the manager added. 'We tried one or two of them on more skilled stuff like machine-moulding, but they did not seem to bed down to it.' The leaders of these groups are sometimes known as 'Big Uncles' and they set a high price on their services to their fellow-countrymen. The 'Big Uncle' often buys a house and brings over a small group of workers. They consider themselves under a strong obligation to him

TABLE IV

Coloured Commonwealth and Colonial Population of Britain Estimates for 1st January, 1959

Country of Origin	
West Indies*	110,000
West Africa†	6000
Pakistan‡	35,000
India§	15,000
Aden and Somaliland†	1500

* Based on British Caribbean Welfare Service Reports.
† Based on 1951 Census Reports.
‡ Estimates from High Commissioner's Office.
§ Author's estimate.

because he helps them with their fares, arranges accommodation, and finds them work. He demands what share of their earnings he wishes. Sometimes he arranges bogus marriages for his charges. Often, it is said, the 'Big Uncle' tightens his hold over his victims by taking away their passports and threatening that the police will deport them if there is any trouble. How much the victims suffer from this system comes to light only when things get bad and work is hard to find; then, thrown out into the street, they may come to somebody for help.

West Indian and West African workers are much too individualistic to tolerate this sort of 'Big Uncle' relationship, and they understand too much of what is going on around them to be liable to such exploitation. They are much less willing to work in a large group of coloured workers as this savours of discrimination, and sometimes prefer to work with a firm employing very few other coloured men so that they will not be blamed for their compatriots' failings. West Indians and Africans are more likely to object to doing work of a character they find personally offensive. A survey by the British Institute of Public Opinion in 1955 showed that 40 per cent of the West Indians interviewed were holding skilled or semi-skilled jobs and 53 per cent unskilled. The remainder were students, housewives, etc. They are reported to have sent postal orders to a value of four and a half million pounds home to Jamaica during 1957.

What have been the British people's reactions to this new wave of immigrants? The overwhelming impression gained from a study of Press reports is of a truly immense amount of activity on the part of local voluntary associations working for better relations. There have been many local inquiries into the difficulties of the immigrants carried out by private individuals in their spare time. Many societies have been formed and committees constituted, even if they have not always achieved very much. Newspapers now report on these topics with much greater sympathy and understanding than ten years ago; any mention of colour discrimination draws a number of protesting letters from readers. There have been many feature articles on the problems of intermarriage, stressing the difficulties but frequently concluding that any girl who appreciates what she would have to contend with, and is nevertheless intent on marrying a coloured man, deserves the support of her kinsfolk and friends.

On the other hand, there have been many cases of hostile behaviour. Some incidents reveal how people can still be ignorant of the most elementary facts, like the landlord who, on agreeing to take a suitable coloured lodger queried: 'Shall I cook his meat or will he have it raw?' In London a skirmish was caused by a woman who objected to a Jamaican's drinking from a public fountain: 'Children have to drink after you,' she protested.

Face-to-face relations between West Indian immigrants and other residents in industrial cities are a jumbled and largely unpredictable mixture of friendliness and veiled hostility. Peter Abrahams, the South African author, has given a personal impression of reactions in Birmingham to the growing coloured population which imparts some of the 'feel' of the situation:

'I hailed a nice-looking young chap near the centre of the town, tried on a West Indian accent and asked for directions to Small Heath. He averted his face, side-stepped and kept moving. I tried another, older man, prosperous-looking. He mumbled something and kept moving.

'I followed a young couple into a tea-place and sat down. No one tried to turn me out. But there were unfriendly stares. I sat at a vacant table. The couple who had gone in just before me were served. Three young men came in and were served. In the end I had to turn and pointedly call the waitress. I got my cup of tea grudgingly, slopping in the saucer. Few migrants would have been as "brash" as I was. I went back to my game of asking directions. One man directed me to what I knew was the wrong bus; a woman raised her nose in the air. Then a young Indian who had seen me snubbed crossed the road and came solicitously to me ... he advised me that it was better to ask directions of coloured people ...

'As the bus sped along the white conductress came round collecting fares. I knew where I wanted to get to but I didn't know how to identify it. Two of my fellow-passengers, both white, came to my rescue and pinpointed it for her. Before he got off one man leaned over and explained to me exactly where to alight. And when I finally got to it the other one tapped me on the shoulder and said: "Your stop, mate."

'Later, I went into a post office. There were only three people ahead of me. The chap behind the counter was tall and gangling, and not long out of his teens. Except for his sneer whenever he looked at me, he seemed nice. Just as the last of the other three people was being served, a fatherly middle-aged gentleman walked in and firmly planted himself in front of me. I straightened up, made a noise in my throat and looked appealingly at the youth. His eyes flickered coldly over my face. Then he turned with the hint of a smile to the middle-aged gentleman. The fatherly type firmly elbowed me out of the way and was served. It needed effort to keep up my pretence then.'³

L

Peter Abrahams's balance of experience was perhaps a shade more unfavourable than the average, and he omits from the picture certain points that could be made on the other side; nevertheless, it is, as he says, the little things that matter in everyday life. To the person who is at the receiving end of this kind of experience day in, day out, it marks him off as someone unwanted. Coloured housewives told Mr Abrahams that they had paid 7s. 6d. for a piece of meat that would have cost an English woman 5s., and he added that the old game of giving strangers short change is not confined to Birmingham.

An African medical student in Glasgow conducted a small experiment regarding the behaviour of conductors on corporation transport. Over a period of nearly a year, 500 journeys were made. In each case he made a note of whether his fare was accepted with thanks or not; he also took a record of whether the conductor thanked the European passenger whose fare was taken just before his, or, if this could not be ascertained, the next passenger after him. In 408 cases both were thanked; in 73, neither; in 19, the European but not the African. In no case was the African the only one to be thanked. It may be that the conductor's responses were automatic; or that there is less discrimination in such matters than in, say, restaurant service; or that the interracial climate is more friendly in a city where the immigrants are primarily students and are few in number. Such questions can be settled and the incidence of discrimination determined only by controlled observation and measurement.

Relations between individual West Indians and Britons in the factories are often very much more friendly than relations between them in the mass. Even between two individuals, however, there are factors which make the establishment of a harmonious relationship more difficult than would normally be the case between two Britons. A perceptive trade union official told Mrs Sheila Patterson: 'Men spend most of their working lives in the factory environment and a feeling of community is evolved. The West Indian is a worse outsider than most. He may be more intelligent: but he often doesn't smoke, he doesn't stand his round of drinks in the near-by pub after work, he may work too hard, he doesn't know or learn the factory gossip or protocol of behaviour, or the accepted forms of swearing. Factory life is a hard one and each newcomer is judged or classified before he realizes it. And in times of unemployment all outsiders are barred. My own Tyneside accent nearly caused a riot in a Birmingham Labour Exchange queue in the early 'thirties ... '

The steady rise in industrial wages after the War left behind wage rates in many forms of municipal employment, such as transport undertakings, fire services, salvage departments, etc. Faced with a growing list of vacancies transport concerns somewhat reluctantly recruited coloured conductors and drivers, West Indians especially. London and Manchester early led the way with small numbers of coloured transport workers, then in 1954 Birmingham Corporation had to recruit them in larger numbers, and in 1955 Sheffield, Nottingham, Coventry and other towns followed suit. Their employment as conductors has done a great deal to improve English understanding of the immigrants and their ways; personal everyday contact has rubbed the strangeness off the newcomers and revealed their cheerfulness and courtesy. Thus when in an East Anglian town recently there was some opposition to West Indians being engaged as bus conductors, a London newspaper commented editorially: 'Londoners are astonished and indeed perplexed to read that in some provincial towns prejudice against coloured transport workers still exists ... The coloured men working on buses, on the Underground and for the Post Office give every satisfaction. They are notably courteous and efficient. The Londoner accepts them without question ... '

The employment of coloured workers in transport undertakings has spotlighted the crucial question of dilution: should they be prevented from monopolizing certain jobs to ensure a smoother integration into the national labour force? On more than one occasion what was felt to be a disproportionate recruitment of coloured workers led to a strike or to official representation from a trade union. Thus in September 1955 Wolverhampton busmen banned overtime working on the demand that coloured staff be kept to a 5 per cent quota. The union spokesman stressed then and later that there was no colour bar but said that the men did not want the staff, then 900 strong including 68 coloureds, to be made up to its full strength of 1050 by the recruitment of more coloured workers. The union had originally agreed to accept 52 coloured and the number should be allowed to fall back to that figure. The union representative denied that his men were trying to keep numbers down so that they could earn more overtime. Unless some action was taken the department would be flooded by coloured people prepared to work for low wages and this would jeopardize the position of the other busmen. Press comment was on the whole sympathetic to the busmen in their desire for economic security and it was appreciated that in a lower-paid occupation workers needed to take on overtime work to maintain their living standards, but nevertheless it was generally agreed that the busmen's proposal was for a colour bar and that such a procedure was abhorrent. Within three weeks the union gave way.

A similar situation developed in Sheffield a year later, when the local branch of the Transport and General Workers' Union sent a deputation to the Corporation Transport Committee with an ultimatum that no further coloured tram conductors should be taken on. This was rejected. The Union spokesman said: 'There is no colour bar and we do not object to coloured labour. At present there are 102 coloured workers on the trams and we feel the limit has been reached. We suggested that no further coloured labour should be engaged. That does not mean that if one leaves he should not be replaced. The normal staff complain that priority and preference is being shown to the coloured staff because of their limitations, and that additional work is being allocated to them.' A no-overtime protest was then called. The union secretary was reported as saying: 'We naturally expect everyone to operate this ban, coloured men as well.' This protest fizzled out. Some newspapers reiterated their view that the workers wanted to restrict recruitment in order to safeguard large overtime earnings. Evidence in support of this view had been provided earlier when bus crews in one Midland town, after a month-long fight against the employment of coloured conductors, had refused to work with university students on vacation, in spite of there being a long list of vacancies for busmen. The evidence indicates, however, that there are more important factors than competition for overtime.

Many workers will say that in the long years of unemployment between the Wars they were told by the employers that their misfortunes were due to the operation of the law of supply and demand in the labour market. Now that this law has at last turned in their favour they see nothing wrong in trying to gain the maximum advantage from the situation. They object that instead of recruiting coloured workers management should raise wages so as to attract local labour. But when there are more jobs than workers and firms are bidding against one another for employees such a policy achieves nothing apart from adding an extra twist to the inflationary spiral. Suspicion of the employers and the financiers of industry underlies much of the workers' recalcitrance, but factors of social prestige may also be involved. The fact that a job can be, and is, done equally well by a coloured man as by a white man is held by many workers to depress its status. If an occupation becomes known as a 'coloured man's job' many whites will wish to leave it and a situation may develop like that of a 'run on the bank' when confidence suddenly snaps and everyone seeks to withdraw at once. In these circumstances there is much to be said for a policy of slow recruitment which enables immigrant labour to be absorbed gradually. The danger is not an imaginary one. When the laying off of motor-trade workers started in the summer of 1956 a reporter waited at the gates and asked one of the first men dismissed what he proposed to do next. The man replied: 'I reckon I will just have to black my face and get a job on the buses.'

Trade union demands for quota restrictions upon the proportion of coloured workers per firm have come from local branches; national executives have never given them public approval. Workers make these demands in their own interests, but it may equally well be held that the spreading of immigrants over many industries and occupations is in the interest of the coloured men as well. In the sense in which the terms have been used in this book, the imposition of a quota cannot be other than a form of discrimination. When it may be considered justifiable is not a question that the sociologist can answer, but it might be held that there is no objection to such a proceeding so long as it is not formalized and inflexible. The arrangement proposed at Sheffield, whereby a certain proportion of jobs were open to coloured men and if one left another would take his place, would involve a radical departure from the principles that have hitherto governed the employment of British subjects.

In the industrial scene at large, colour discrimination is not infrequent, but as in other spheres there is much variation and some workers experience very little. After an incident which had attracted wide attention a Nigerian volunteered a statement to a Middlesborough newspaper because, he said, he was anxious that Britain should not be misrepresented abroad. He was a labourer at a local steel works who had lived in Britain since 1940, was married to a Canadian girl and owned his own house. He said: 'As far as I am concerned, there is no colour bar at all in this country. Britain is the only country under the sun where Negroes have the freedom and the right to work side by side with white people and organize their own affairs without hindrance ... I get fairer treatment here even than in my native country ... I have many white friends. We drink from the same glass and eat from the same dish. We work in brotherhood ... In other countries the insiders get the best of everything. In this country the outsider gets a fair chance. But if I read reports coming out from Britain to my own country I would think there was a colour bar.' Yet the Nigerian's view is not shared by most of his fellows, and the incident which gave rise to his intervention suggests a very different state of affairs. A Jamaican and a Pakistani labourer had been sent to join a gang laying a water main, but the men there would not allow the newcomers to work with them. The Jamaican sent his war service medals back to Buckingham Palace saying they no longer meant anything to him. Newspaper reporters interviewed the men involved and quoted the Jamaican as saying: 'I had to leave my last job as boilerman because of the men ... I have no quarrel with the management of industry – it's the men. Is it the men and the unions who are running the industries?' One of the white workers who had objected to him was quoted as saying that he would 'stick to his guns' even if the union threatened to expel him, and he would certainly consider joining the newly formed British branch of the Ku-Klux-Klan which was then much in the news. 'I am not one of those,' he said, 'who maintain that all blacks should be murdered, but I firmly believe they should be sent back home. If that can't be done they should be made to live in one particular part of all towns and their children should not be able to go to the same school as white children.' The employers afterwards made strong representations about this incident to the Transport and General Workers' Union, but the position of the local union leader is not easy when he has to implement a policy opposed to the wishes of union members.

The trade unions have never been enthusiastic about any of the schemes for bringing foreign workers to Britain, for they fear that this can only lead to a worsening in their own position. Resistance is likely to be all the stronger when, as in the case of the West Indians, the immigrants are readily recognized as newcomers. Union leaders have never been able to make up their minds firmly as to where their strongest loyalties lie. They have felt on the one hand that they have a duty to the immigrants who are workers like themselves: they must be protected from exploitation or from being used as tools for the exploitation of others. On the other hand, union leaders have felt that they have strong duties to their 'own' folk whose interests were threatened by the influx of competitors. Thus most unions have failed to agree upon and make effective any policy for laying off workers in the event of unemployment. Was it to be 'last in, first out', or were the best workers to be kept till last irrespective of length of service? Many of the rank and file took it for granted that the coloured men should go first, whatever the circumstances. Thus there was considerable apprehension when workers in the Midlands motor factories were laid off and a general recession threatened. In January 1956 there were 600 unemployed coloured workers in Birmingham and the situation was said to be hardening, but by August there was still said to be no more than 700, many of these being recent arrivals. Discharged coloured workers had moved fairly readily to the north-west where there was a surplus of vacancies. In September an official spokesman said that in the country as a whole there were about 6800 unemployed coloured people, an increase of about 1500 in three months. In the same period the total number of coloured workers in employment had risen by 6000 (which suggested that the level of unemployment was not high, bearing in mind the fact that it would include many migrants who had only recently landed). The speaker said that inquiries by the National Assistance Board had shown that there was no 'hard core' of unemployed coloured workers. [4] The Government attached great importance to the freedom of all British citizens to come freely into the country and he thought it unnecessary to stress what a far-reaching step it would be for the Government to introduce legislation to restrict this freedom. By the February of the following year unemployment amongst coloured males in the Birmingham area had fallen slightly and with the revival of trade the danger was soon over. Yet the spell of uncertainty had been long enough to cause bitterness. White workers saw unemployment as the only way of forcing the coloured men home, and the immigrants spoke of an ebbing of the friendliness of their white fellow-workers who sometimes became hostile towards any coloured man kept on at the expense of a white worker.

Surveying the broad outlines of the employment position, one of the salient features is the importance of leadership if coloured workers are to be introduced successfully into an existing concern. The white workers' collective attitude is one of marked caution. If a trade union official regards himself as no more than the representative of his branch members, and consults with them when the management raises the question of introducing coloured workers, the result will probably be unfavourable and friction will follow. If he sees himself as a leader and has the ability to drive the issue through, it may appear no problem at all. Similarly where management is concerned. Studies of relations in industry agree that when a go-ahead manager determines to introduce coloured workers and supervises their induction there is little opposition. In a sphere of uncertainty and conflicting inclinations determined leadership in either direction is decisive. Thus Miss Janet Reid has reported that in an engineering factory a departmental manager told one of his men that he was to work with a coloured man and teach him the job. 'I'm not working with a black so-and-so,' the man said.

'You *are*,' replied the manager. A few months later the white man was still working at the same machine with the coloured man as his mate, and was said to be 'fussing over him like an old hen'.[5] In some firms whites and coloureds work together in great harmony and good temper. What is the secret? There is none. The firms that get on well with coloured immigrants are the firms that get on well with their own workers. A little more understanding and flexibility may be needed, but the principles of good personnel management are just the same.

Apart from employment the other chief sphere in which immigration has given rise to difficulty is that of housing. Many houses were destroyed by bombing during the war and despite rapid reconstruction the supply of dwellings has never been anywhere near to meeting the demand. Partly this is because with rising standards of living people are no longer content with conditions that would earlier have been tolerated. In part the seriousness of the situation derives from the disproportionate industrial expansion and population increase of particular towns, such as in the Birmingham region. When British people have been many years on the waiting list for rehousing they resent the competition from immigrants. The overcrowding and poor conditions in many houses bought by immigrants make people fear the spread of infection and they complain about the general decline in neighbourhood standards.

In 1956 the public health staff of the county borough of West Bromwich carried out a survey.[6] Most of the 72 houses there which had been bought by coloured people were of the larger Victorian type suitable for sub-letting; 15 of the houses were of very poor construction and it was believed that several of them had been bought at prices above their market value. There were 505 West Indian residents, and 333 Indians and Pakistanis; but whereas 27 houses were owned by West Indians, 45 were owned by Indians and Pakistanis, many of whom took in West Indian lodgers. Washing facilities, refuse storage and living standards generally were found to be inferior to those of the average English family, but, having regard to all the circumstances, not seriously so. Tuberculosis appeared to occur most commonly among Indians living in the most overcrowded conditions. The investigators found no evidence that coloured immigrants suffering from active tuberculosis had come to the borough, the one West Indian case having been that of a man born in the United Kingdom. The standard of child care in coloured people's homes was found to be quite satisfactory.

The most notable attempts to deal with coloured immigrants' housing difficulties have come from the formation of special housing societies. These have been set up in a number of cities on the initiative of sympathetic white residents, and their achievements in raising capital and in organization are impressive. The first of these societies, Aggrey Housing Ltd., was formed in Leeds early in 1955; by the end of the following year it owned 51 dwellings in Leeds and London. The society had rehoused 30 families, mostly African and West Indian, but also Indian, Polish, Latvian and Austrian, and had assisted a further 42 families to buy their own homes. Their example has been followed in Birmingham, Bath, Nottingham, Sheffield and Derby, while similar action has been proposed in several other cities.

Shortage of housing is probably one of the most important factors contributing to hostility towards West Indians in districts of dense settlement. Many West Indians have bought their own houses in neighbourhoods where property values have been falling, often large houses which have been let out in flats. But under legislation surviving from the war they are not allowed to give notice to tenants of unfurnished property without offering them alternative accommodation. Wishing to obtain the use of the rooms, so that they can let them to their own people and obtain higher rents for the repayment of the mortgage, the new owners make themselves as unpleasant as possible until the sitting tenants leave of their own accord. Nor are the neighbours pleased when the house is overcrowded with immigrants who are often given to noisy musical parties and are not always worried about observing the local conventions.

We mentioned in Chapter V that informal controls are weaker in districts near the bottom of the social scale, so that there is a greater tolerance of unorthodox conduct. This is equally true, and for similar reasons, in areas of changing social character. It is therefore easy to appreciate why the disturbances of September 1958 occurred in parts of North Kensington and Nottingham where West Indian settlement was of relatively recent date, and not in Cardiff or Liverpool where residents have become used to coloured people and community controls have been re-established. The informal controls which in more settled neighbourhoods ensure the observance of local proprieties are weak in districts like Notting Hill, so that when the situation appears to be getting out of hand the residents' only remaining sanction is the resort to violence.

To judge by Press reports and the recent account of the disorders prepared by Mr James Wickenden, in both Nottingham and North Kensington the white residents were exasperated by the conduct of a minority of the coloured immigrants. Because they could not themselves bring pressure to bear upon this group they put the pressure upon the whole coloured community. The disturbances were widely described as 'race riots', an expression which may cause people to overlook the fact that no one was killed, and no one — apparently — seriously disabled. In Nottingham, irritation centred on the activities of a group of 'wide boys' who carried knives and organized prostitution, and it was aggravated by their aggressive behaviour in the employment exchange. Late on August the twenty-third a minor altercation outside a public house caused crowds to gather. Within a few minutes West Indians had produced knives and stabbed six Englishmen. Coloured people have testified, however, that the fighting was between mixed groups, and not black versus white. Popular feeling mounted instantaneously, but the police dispersed crowds and by midnight all was quiet. During the week a new element was introduced. One newspaper reported that Teddy boys, armed with knives, were patrolling the district and serving as 'self-appointed guardians of the peace'. The following Saturday the neighbourhood was full of irresponsible youths from outside the district, and considerable numbers of adult sightseers. A similar crowd gathered again the next week, but the police were gradually able to get matters back to normal.

There had been several minor racial incidents in the Notting Hill district of North Kensington during the summer of 1958, three of them on the same night as that of the trouble in Nottingham. The first major clash occurred seven days later and the newspaper publicity given to the idea of Teddy boys acting as vigilantes may have been influential here also. The Teddy boys had previously been regarded with distaste by their elders but now they were seen as local heroes enforcing neighbourhood standards and were thus egged on to stir up fresh trouble. Feeling against the immigrants derived partly from a minority's involvement in commercial prostitution, and partly from habits of theirs which some residents thought outrageous. The coloured men failed to keep up appearances. They sat outside on the balconies which fringe many of the decaying houses, and sometimes sat there with bare feet. They did not always put up curtains. They shouted, and held late-night parties with the radiogram at full blast. White resentment over such matters seems to have been an important element in the support temporarily given to hooligans and trouble-seeking adolescents.

Just as the whites in poor, transitional neighbourhoods of this kind find themselves without the means of enforcing their conventions, so the immigrants are denied the social support they might obtain in more settled areas. West Indians in both districts felt that they did not get sufficient assistance from the police and that they must look to their own defence. Finding that some whites were ready to exploit them if given the opportunity, they adopted an aggressive outlook as being the best policy in circumstances where victory went to the strong.

It would appear that there was some anti-Negro propaganda and agitation in North Kensington, and that right-wing extremists attempted to exploit popular sentiment just after the disturbances, but it is doubtful if fascist activities played any major part in the events. The tinder was there; only the match was required. Nor can blame for the disorders be attributed to the unenlightenment of the white residents, their lack of education or their faulty understanding of the brotherhood of man. When questions of race are involved the conduct of educated people and men of high moral principle has not always been above reproach. It is probable that any other group of Britons placed in the same situation as the whites of these districts would have behaved in a similar manner.

The slenderness of the support which has been accorded to fascist and extremist organizations reinforces the view that the improvement of relations is not hindered by the unfavourable attitudes of Britons as individuals. Even if the proportion of people holding strongly anti-coloured sentiments is less than four in a hundred, this is still a considerable group in the total adult population. Many minority organizations attain national importance with a much smaller following. Yet up to the end of 1958 no political organization had made any serious attempt to capitalize latent hostility. The Union Movement — successor to the British Union of Fascists — had gained some notoriety for the slogan 'Keep Britain White', the initials KBW being sometimes painted on walls near areas of coloured settlement. But this organization has been too much discredited to gain any continuous support. Leaders of the League of Empire Loyalists have declared that coloured immigration should be halted, but they have concentrated their attacks upon the policy of giving colonies independence and have not tried to make much of the domestic issue. In the case of both these organizations, however, the rank and file may be more hostile towards the immigrants than the party statements. The only avowedly anti-coloured agitation has been in the name of the Ku-Klux-Klan. In April 1957 a newspaper disclosed that this organization had opened a branch in Britain and had printed membership forms for Britons to join 'the Aryan Knights, Ku-Klux-Klan realm of Britain and Texas'. When exposed to considerable publicity at the hands of reporters who were patently unsympathetic, the organizer lost confidence and claimed that his real intention had been to attack Communists in the trade unions. The alarm aroused by news of this attempt and the mobilization of liberal opinion in more recent months suggest that it would be almost impossible at present for any openly racialist organization to gain a significant following in Britain.

Part IV

THE MEANING OF COLOUR

CHAPTER X

QUOD ERAT DEMONSTRANDUM

It's you whites who make us coloured.   BRITISH-BORN COLOURED WOMAN

IN the first three chapters we set out a general view of the scientific problems posed by relations between people of different background and experience. A full justification of this approach would be out of place in this volume and many of its implications must be passed over. Those which are of chief importance to the argument may be expressed in the form of three theses:

A1. *That prejudice and discrimination are different aspects of behaviour and require different explanations.*

A2. *Discrimination is to be seen as the outcome of situations in which a class of persons is considered to have different rights and obligations from others, and not as the expression of individual sentiments.*

A3. *The rights and obligations of parties to a relationship are expressed in norms of conduct which may either be explicit in the laws of the land, or implicit in customary ways of behaving.*

These are not propositions that can be proved, but are assumptions underlying a particular mode of inquiry. If their adoption can lead to satisfactory solutions their value is clear. In the present case it may be claimed that a sociological theory starting from the concept of the person provides more useful results than those based on slippery notions of 'society', 'culture', 'group', etc., which are favoured by most of the dreary textbooks of sociology now current.

Ideas as to the rights and obligations of particular classes of people change over time. The same actors come to be regarded as different social persons. A cursory review of British conceptions of the coloured man during the past two centuries suggests:

B1. *That by the early years of the twentieth century the relationship between Britons and coloured colonials had developed into one in which Britons were thought to be socially and morally superior to their charges and responsible for their upbringing. Britons claimed rights consonant with their assumed obligations and expected colonials to conduct themselves as subordinates.*

B2. *In recent years the old norms have lost their validity, largely owing to the refusal of coloured people to enter into relations on these terms.*

The political and social problems associated with racial differences are becoming increasingly complex.[1] People who are involved in everyday dealings with stranger groups have difficulty in putting their finger on just what it is that causes the friction. To abuse them for not understanding that old-style racialism is dead, and why it is dead, only makes them feel that it is no use trying to explain. If instead we are to explore the changes in people's expectations of one another which are the critical elements in inter-group friction, the historian's co-operation is needed.

In Chapters V and VI we have considered British social life as maintained by the rights and obligations of persons to one another; we discussed the difficulties arising from the introduction of actors not familiar with them, and from Britons' uncertainty as to the rights of the immigrants. Our main theses in this section are four in number. Owing to the lack of first-hand reporting of face-to-face relations between white and coloured people we have not always been able to defend them convincingly; but in any event, to obtain a reliable indication of their validity it would be necessary to undertake a new empirical investigation bearing just these points in mind.

C1. *That in any society the network of social relations is maintained by common agreement about the behaviour appropriate to particular relationships. Strangers are people who are unaware of these norms of conduct. The coloured man is considered the most distant of all strangers.*

Thus we have held that the social difference between whites and coloureds in Britain is conceived as a difference of degree and not of kind. Behaviour towards coloured people is not radically different from all other sorts of behaviour but accentuates features discernible in relations between Britons of different class or regional background, or between Britons and white foreigners. There are certain possible exceptions to this principle, notably in circumstances where fundamental norms of sexual behaviour are in question, but the view of the coloured man as a non-person is restricted to such situations and does not carry over to more usual relationships. The suggestion that Britons rely more than most nations on unspoken norms of conduct casts new light upon our famous lack of enthusiasm for foreigners generally, and deserves further consideration. Certainly it is to be expected that the more a nation depends upon tacit understandings about behaviour the more difficult will it be for a newcomer to learn what these understandings are; while in the case of coloureds mutual adjustment is hindered by Britons' ignorance of the immigrants' background and aspirations.

C2. *Custom earlier prescribed that coloured men had different rights and obligations from white men; this has now been discarded as a general guide to conduct without any agreement having yet been reached as to the principle that is to replace it.*

The general uncertainty about the right way to treat coloured people underlies much of the unpredictability of race relations in Britain. People are bewildered not about the rightness of particular moral principles but about their relevance to particular situations. Should they be just and treat coloured immigrants on a basis of complete equality with whites, or should they be charitable and give them special consideration? How far does justice require charity? How far may charity go before it becomes patronage? When is discrimination wrong? The fascination of the racial scene in present-day Britain is that a new agreement as to the correct way of reconciling these principles is in the making. One of the sociologists' chief contributions is to clarify the factors which cause people to regard coloured immigrants as a separate category of persons and hinder them from treating them the same as white people.

C3. *Relations between Britons and coloured people cannot yet be assimilated to the pattern of relations between Britons:*

  (a) *because coloured men are believed to be unfamiliar with the norms by which these relations are governed and the ways in which the parties convey to each other their expectations and interpretations;*

  (b) *because a dark skin colour detracts from a man's prestige, and, where the nature of the relationship is not generally recognized or approved, from the prestige of those who are seen associating with him.*

C4. *Owing to the ambiguities as to the proper course of conduct, Britons are apt to avoid entering into relations with coloured people. Avoidance is most marked in relationships based upon implicit norms and in which sanctions upon deviant behaviour are weak.*

When one man sells another a motor car it does not matter whether the two of them understand each other's sentiments regarding the sale. But if this is to be one in a series of transactions then the non-contractual elements acquire a special importance. If the seller drives a hard bargain over one particular car the buyer may expect him to be more lenient the next time. If he is not, then the seller may lose a customer. The same is true of most social relationships: if the parties cannot understand each other's interpretations of what goes on, the relationship will break down and the participants will be reluctant to enter into similar relationships with other people unless they can be sure of this mutual understanding. A white man may fear that if he does a coloured man a favour the latter may take this as something to which he is entitled. Coloured workers may conclude that it is no use trying to explain their point of view and that the only course is to become aggressive when confronted with actions of which they disapprove. Among such hindrances to effective communication is the coloured man's lack of easily discerned status symbols. All coloured men are thought to look alike and the professional man is not easily recognized from the recent immigrant, or the good worker from the scrounger. These obstacles to understanding are not dissolved by attempts to ignore them, but neither are they an argument for keeping the groups separate. Inter-group understanding is slowly built up by mutual acquaintance and the process can be hastened by conscious acts of policy.

To suggest that all coloured colonials are thought of as socially inferior to all Britons would be to invest these social categories with a significance they could never maintain in practice. A coloured doctor is not ranked below a white shop assistant, nor an African chief below a typist. But unless he is known to be better qualified or more competent a coloured doctor will not be considered fully the equal of his white colleague. The coloured man always has to go one better to obtain an equal position. The negative significance of a dark skin colour for social prestige may also be transferred to those who identify themselves with coloured men by association.

Propositions C1 to C4 constitute the most plausible explanation of our four initial paradoxes that can be constructed from the data available. We have shown that British conduct towards coloured people cannot be explained as the outcome of prejudice, because Britons have often responded very generously to the difficulties created by the recent influx, while individual Britons are very well disposed towards the immigrants. There is discrimination, some in the coloured people's favour, much to their disfavour; the latter does not represent an attempt to confine the immigrants to a subordinate role in the national life but is a form of the avoidance of strangers that can be discerned in almost any society. As might be expected this avoidance is most marked in private relationships. Custom provides no general formula as to the proper course of action and indicators as to the status-rights of particular coloured men are few. Hence any new piece of information, even one so slight that no weight would be placed on it in relations with fellow-Britons, may cause the actor to redefine the situation and to behave in a quite different manner. Finally, individual Britons' beliefs that their fellows are less favourably disposed towards coloured people than they are themselves can be understood once the independence of group norms from individual attitudes is appreciated.

Similar propositions might prove useful in other situations where relations between groups are marked by avoidance and uncertainty rather than by hostility. The position of Jews in Britain, for example, resembles in some respects that of coloured people. There is very little outright hostility towards Jews but they are made to keep their distance; they are often excluded from golf clubs and similar organizations and there is little doubt that most people prefer to associate with Gentiles where possible. Jews are also strangers in many social circles. It may be that while rejecting anti-Semitism Gentiles feel they cannot treat Jews in quite the same fashion for reasons similar to those operative in the case of coloured people. Again, there are certain resemblances with the position of Negroes in some of the northern parts of the United States. They complain they can rarely be certain how whites will behave towards them; segregation has been abolished without acceptance taking its place.[2] These parallels might repay closer examination.

Our material also suggests certain other propositions about race relations in Britain which may be recalled in conclusion:

D1. *That coloured men form a social group only in response to dis-crimination on the part of the whites.*

Where outside pressure is absent, Asians, Africans and coloured Americans are chiefly aware only of the differences between them, both in customs and shades of colouring. They are made conscious that they have a distinctive characteristic only by the realization that they share a common experience — that of being treated in a special way by whites. 'The coloured man' is a creation of Europeans.

D2. *Despite the tendency to regard 'coloured workers' as one category, group relations are structured by the rights claimed and the obliga-tions observed by the immigrants.*

We have shown that the West Africans and West Indians on the one hand, and the Indians and Pakistanis on the other, have radically differ-ent aspirations and ways of responding to settlement in Britain.

Jamaicans claim social equality to a much greater extent than Pakistanis; they are also willing to observe the obligations of citizenship much more than are Pakistanis, most of whom avoid becoming more involved in British ways than is necessary. The Jamaican and Pakistani worker are thus different social persons and Britons are forced, unwittingly at times, to recognize this by behaving towards them in different fashions.

We have demonstrated that the pattern of collective behaviour on the part of Britons cannot be understood as a response to the biological characteristics of coloured men, nor as the acting out of the sentiments of individual Britons. The significance attached to the physical characteristics of a stranger group is largely the outcome of the parties' views of each other's customary rights and obligations. Problems of this order fall within the sphere of sociological theory, and, apart from jurisprudence, within no other. We do not seek to deny that the psychological and economic aspects of the situation under discussion are of importance, or that in certain overseas situations political, demographic, geographical and other elements may be of central significance. But it does appear that in relations between white and coloured people in Britain the sociological factors are sometimes the decisive ones.

It has sometimes been objected that social situations occur in a historical context; that we cannot understand them out of that context, and that therefore any sociological generalizations must be restricted to particular historical periods. This is not the case. As we have argued, the sociologist does not attempt to comprehend the whole phenomenon but only an aspect of it, and then in terms of analytical categories. If he postulates some sort of association between lineage organization and age sets, or between strong ties of kinship and the weakness of the State's authority, these are not falsified by the discovery of periods or societies where age sets or state organization are unknown.[3]

For the coloured man his colour means that he is set apart from ordinary Britons. Occasionally the gulf between them closes up and he can share in the pleasures and the grumbles of white comrades. In such situations his colour has been forgotten; no longer does it have any social significance. This happens only rarely, for the coloured man is likely to reflect that sooner or later something will occur to remind him of his feelings of solidarity with other coloured people and the opposition of the whites in general. Though the immigrant may become assimilated to a small group in which his individual qualities are appreciated this does not avail him in circumstances where these qualities are unknown or are denied. He has in the past been regarded as a permissible scapegoat upon whom people might vent their discontents, and in times of trouble he has been reclassified as a stranger who never really belonged at all.

The Briton's conception of the coloured men has been changing rapidly. The transformation of the political relationship between Britain and her colonies and former colonies has much to do with this. So, too, has the ordinary Briton's growing acquaintance with coloured immigrants in his everyday life. Familiarity banishes fear. At the present time Britons' behaviour towards coloured people is ambiguous. Their avoidance of them is, however, a natural response to social situations in which colour in varying degrees means strangeness, unreliability, involvement in unfamiliar problems, raised eyebrows on the neighbours' part and a reputed disregard for the sexual inhibitions of the British way of life.

Appendix I

TEN COMMANDMENTS
OF INTER-GROUP RELATIONS

TEN COMMANDMENTS
OF INTER-GROUP RELATIONS

Nor is it for want of admirable doctrines that men hate, despise, censure,
deceive and subjugate one another.   PERCY BYSSHE SHELLEY[1]

WHAT is lacking for the improvement of group relations in
Britain is not goodwill. Nor is there any deficiency of
moralizing. We have shown that the difficulties are not to any
significant extent the outgrowth of an irrational force deep down in
the individual psyche — a view which leads some people to argue that
prejudice is something which, regrettably, will always be with us and
about which there is little that we can do. On the contrary we have
held that social factors can hamstring individual goodwill; that British
behaviour towards the immigrants is a rational response to the customary meaning of colour, and that custom can be changed by conscious
policy.

The coloured nations are beginning to set the pace in racial relationships. They make new demands upon British conduct, and, as the world
balance of power shifts, Britons are forced to comply. Held back by the
bonds of custom their readjustment is reluctant — some would say
dangerously slow. Cannot changes in custom be accelerated? In recent
years there have been many investigations in the United States which
bear upon this question. Their results have been brought together in
John P. Dean's and Alex Rosen's *A Manual of Intergroup Relations*, where
the authors' conclusions are embodied in a series of twenty-seven propositions about the likely effects of particular policies and actions. We
have selected those most relevant to the British situation and com-
pressed them where possible, to leave ten principles which, always
assuming the continuation of favourable political and economic
tendencies, can most help to promote inter-group harmony.[2]

PROPOSITION I. *The more frequently members of the two groups meet one another in everyday situations the more friendly will relations between them be.*

It has been found that the less contact people of a district have with strangers the more suspicious they are of them. Country people are disturbed by the arrival of a foreigner because they have little experience of meeting foreigners in their normal activities. Introduce a few coloured bus conductors, postmen, barmen or workers in the public eye and relations will improve. Personal learning leads to the abandonment of misconceptions in a way that formal instruction never can, but it is brought about indirectly. For most people mutual understanding is achieved not by bringing them together with this aim in view but by their working together in pursuit of common objectives.

PROPOSITION 2. *Clumsiness in interpersonal relations spoils the best intentions.*

Remarks which to the Englishman sound unexceptional may give offence to the coloured man. The former may use epithets like 'nigger', 'wog' and 'Sambo' in all innocence, but his doing so will anger any coloured man or put him so ill at ease that friendly relations will be well-nigh impossible. Innocence of intent on the white man's part is not acceptable as a justification for their use. Many such terms and notions unfavourable to coloured men are propagated by children's books and by nursery rhymes, some of which will have eventually to be revised (children learn just as happily to recite 'Eeny meeny miney mo, catch a tiger by the toe ... '). As some publishers consider that the caricaturing of other races in children's books is a matter of no significance, a closer investigation of the question might be of value. One expression that is to be avoided, less perhaps because it may give offence than because it is a prop to slovenly thinking, is the phrase 'colour problem'. This word 'problem' is often used to cover what might otherwise be regarded as a multitude of sins. Has South Africa a race problem? One might as well ask whether Russia, in November 1956, had a 'Hungarian problem'. The expression implies that it is colour which creates the problem, and encourages people to think that if the immigrants went away all would be well. But would not this be to leave the source of the trouble untouched? Would it not be more accurate to say that we are confronted with a 'white problem'?

In trying to strike up relations with coloured people Britons may also offer testimonials of a tactless character, like a former colonial civil servant's harping on the virtues of illiterate tribal Africans to a young nationalist impatient for the modernization of his country. The person who with a self-conscious and half-ashamed note in his voice asks the colonial student 'Excuse my asking, but where do you come from?' shows that he recognizes the conventional practice of patronage while only half accepting it, and giving the student no clear indication of the terms on which he is offering his temporary friendship. Some people are aware of this difficulty: they feel that if they try to be friendly with a coloured man he will guess that they are doing so because he is coloured, and will resent it. Those who are less sensitive to these under-tones of interpretation know no such inhibitions. Hence yet another paradox: that it is often the least understanding Britons with whom coloured immigrants come into contact. Those who appreciate such difficulties should not conclude that the attempt is not worth making: they are far more likely to overcome them than people who have not realized they exist.

Discussion of such obstacles prompts a more general reflection and a parallel with psychoanalysis. It would probably be agreed that the most valuable *general* contribution psychoanalysis has made (therapy for individuals being a separate consideration) is the insight it has given people into their motives and the workings of the unconscious. This enables them to act with a fuller understanding of the psychological forces at work. Similarly, the insight which the sociological analysis of face-to-face relationships can provide helps people to appreciate better the structure of the situations in which they are caught up and to act with a deeper understanding of them.

PROPOSITION 3. *Understanding between groups is impeded by ignoring individual and group differences and treating all persons as though they were alike.*

It is sometimes said that the best inter-group policy is no policy; that social differences can be abolished if only people will ignore them. But the 'treat-everybody-alike' theory is applicable only within restricted circumstances. Jews, for example, have different holidays and food habits which others may reasonably be asked to respect. A member of an ill-favoured minority will have many recollections of occasions when he and his fellows have been maltreated. He will not respond to someone who seeks to discount this experience as irrelevant. If minorities suffer from discrimination it is impracticable to overlook this; furthermore, they may have their own contributions to make to the life of the host country and the cultivation of their special abilities may bring them a counterbalancing esteem.

PROPOSITION 4. *Any committee or similar body concerned with relations between whites and coloureds must include at least two genuine leaders of the coloured group.*

Any committee which does not do this will be regarded by immigrants as a body attempting to manipulate them to suit the convenience of the majority. Coloured representatives should be sought not just as spokesmen for 'their' people, but also as responsible members of the community as well able to take decisions in the interests of the whole as any other member of the committee. They can provide the others with factual information, explain their fellows' feelings and why they react in ways the majority finds strange, and can do more to ensure support from the minority than anyone else. There must be more than one minority representative so that their followers may have some check upon anything said in their name; neither of them will retire into polite acquiescence if he must maintain his role as a champion of minority rights in the eyes of a fellow minority member. When there is more than one they may be able to reinforce one another's views, or, by disagreeing, to show variations of opinion within the minority. If an interracial body is to be effective it must choose as minority representatives people who are genuine leaders of the minority no matter, within reason, what their occupation, party politics or personal reputation. All too often people are apt to protest: 'Oh, but we couldn't possibly have *him* on the committee — why, the man's utterly irresponsible.' The man in question may be the only one trusted by the minority and able to speak on their behalf. Usually the host society makes the immigrant leader what he is. If they treat with him his position is strengthened and he can sometimes commit his followers to courses of which they are suspicious. If the host society will not have any dealings with him he is driven to more and more bitter and 'extremist' protests to retain his followers. The less recognition is given to minority leaders the more difficult does it become to find one whom the majority think worthy of recognition. In Britain, coloured protest leaders are apt to claim that until the colonies are independent harmonious relations between whites and coloured are impossible. This does not mean that they will not readily assist in short-term schemes intended to benefit their fellows.

PROPOSITION 5. *People tend to accept and perpetuate customary ways of behaving towards minority members irrespective of their personal inclinations. If new customary practices of a more favourable character appear to be accepted by most people then individuals will accept them themselves, and newcomers will conform to the practices prevailing.*

When in Rome, do as Rome does. Visitors usually follow this advice, if not from choice then of necessity. The South African who would insist on racial segregation in his own country realizes that he cannot expect it in Britain. Public bodies can create new and more equitable customs within their own sphere of operation and the norms established there will spread to other sectors. Governmental bodies, employers, unions and voluntary associations can do most in this respect, but the principle can also be applied on a smaller scale.

PROPOSITION 6. *Determined leaders can establish practices that would be resisted were they introduced in a halting fashion.*

This proposition follows from the preceding. If a works manager who wishes to introduce coloured workers holds a ballot on the subject he will draw out the least favourable responses, whereas by giving the impression that engaging coloured men is nothing in any way strange or unconventional he may impose his definition of the situation upon others. Of course, this is no licence for autocracy, for someone who is out of touch with popular sentiment and tries to force through too radical a measure may destroy whatever limited advances have earlier been gained.

PROPOSITION 7. *Objectionable behaviour should be publicly challenged, with an explanation of why it is not acceptable; the person challenged should, if possible, be helped to understand that the criticism is of a way of behaving and not of himself as an individual.*

If objectionable behaviour is allowed to pass unchallenged people will conclude that others sympathize with it. If the fear of what others think is to be banished it is essential that liberal opinion be made explicit. In criticizing unfriendly behaviour, however, it is important to indicate what is wrong; to suggest that the person criticized is personally evil or stupid will force him into defending and perpetuating such practices. The importance of expressing criticism tactfully is a matter of every-day experience. To bring conflicts into the open is not necessarily to exacerbate them; if they can be successfully resolved this is often a starting-point for a further move towards improving relations.

PROPOSITION 8. *It is often advisable to try first to get different parties to agree to fair-play policies, and then afterwards to press for their implementation.*

A step-by-step approach has much to commend it. If, for example, union and management leaders can be persuaded to agree in times of full employment to fair-play policies for laying-off in the event of redundancy, then the chances of avoiding discrimination if redundancy later occurs are much better.

PROPOSITION 9. *In forming interracial organizations it is important to secure the support of the more powerful leaders of the white community and not to depend heavily on the type of person referred to in America as the 'interracial duty delegate'.*

There is the danger that civic, industrial and union leaders may not play a part commensurate with their community responsibilities because the planning of inter-group programmes has come to be regarded as the work of particular sorts of people.

PROPOSITION 10. *Attempts to modify discriminatory behaviour are unlikely to be successful unless they counter the social pressures that give rise to such practices.*

A little example can be worth more than a lot of preaching, but example itself will not be of much avail where the interests of the two groups are opposed to one another. However, it is not in the interests of the nation that the two groups should be allowed ever to take up antagonistic positions. It may be held that just as the Government has been forced to intervene in disputes between powerful sections of the body politic, so it should declare discrimination on grounds of race or colour illegal. The argument in favour of this has been set out by a number of speakers and writers, but it is still misconstrued.[3] People opposed to the suggestion often appear to regard the law as an expression of the common will and to object to its use as a deliberate means of changing behaviour (though no objection is raised on this score to traffic safety legislation). They sometimes take the view that anti-discrimination legislation is a step in the direction of prescribing by law what people shall think. This betrays a fundamental misunderstanding. There are many cranks and societies of cranks, who are harmless so long as they do not attempt to put their views in practice. Similarly, there is no harm in individuals holding fascist opinions so long as they do not attempt to mount anti-parliamentary campaigns or to subvert the Government. People may continue to think coloured people inferior beings, just as others advocate polygamy or unrestricted legalized abortion. But if they attempt to put their beliefs into effect then there must be legislation to provide for their punishment and the compensation of those who have suffered by their actions. A colour-bar law would have considerable value in demonstrating national disapproval of racial discrimination. Only in a relatively few cases would the issues be clear enough to justify their being taken to the courts, but the securing of just one or two convictions would have profound effect. Such legislation would not create a class of privileged persons, for the publican could still exclude a particular coloured customer on other grounds and he could still make him feel unwelcome, but it would reduce discrimination against coloured people as a class. Customary practices supported by the fear that 'other people might object' lag behind individual opinion. Legislation is the most effective way of bringing them into line; it is a proper instrument of policy in a sphere such as this where formal education is of very little help.

It has earlier been suggested that attempts to instruct members of the majority group in schoolroom fashion about the immigrants as people with problems not unlike their own would have little effect upon relations between the groups. No one will warm to his coloured brother if he feels he is being 'got at' by the teacher. Yet there is much to be said, as a background measure having effect in the long-run, for any attempt to educate the general British public as to the true character of the Commonwealth and its possibilities, for there is no chance of the ideal of a multi-racial commonwealth ever becoming a reality unless members of the working public learn more about and show more interest in the affairs of present and former colonies. In this connection it is worthwhile repeating the peroration with which the P.E.P. group concluded its study: 'One side of the problem is outside the province of the various bodies connected with the education and welfare of the colonial student. This is the complete indifference of the British public to their own great colonial inheritance. Perhaps it is natural for an island people to set little store by the opinions and customs of foreigners, but when the same insularity is applied to the inhabitants of colonial territories the dangers are obvious. The level of ignorance described in this inquiry remains as a standing reproach to the British educational system.'

BRITISH RACIAL ATTITUDES

BRITISH RACIAL ATTITUDES

Half the trouble in this world is because of not being used to things!
ALCESTER HOUSEWIFE

THE attitude survey was planned at the beginning of our study in order to obtain a rough idea of how the general population felt towards coloured people. This information was needed as a check on the impressions given by the various local studies, which suggested a stronger and more general antipathy than our own experiences would have indicated. It was not intended to investigate variations in disposition associated with age, income, occupation, etc., though information was collected on these points in case the overall pattern should be seriously affected by such variations. In the light of the theory advanced earlier it would appear that any future inquiry might profitably ascertain what are considered to be the coloured man's rights and obligations in situations of various types.

Three hundred people were interviewed during August and September 1956. Fifty were chosen at random from the electoral rolls in each of six localities: Ipswich, Coventry, Alcester (a rural district in Warwickshire), Leeds, Hawick (Roxburghshire) and Leith. Throughout the survey the procedures used by the governmental Social Survey were adhered to. Great care was taken lest there should be a tendency for the people refusing to be interviewed to include a disproportionate number of those holding unpopular opinions and unwilling to disclose them to a stranger. The interviewers implied that their questions were mostly about the colonies — as the opening ones were — and ascertained as carefully as possible the motives and opinions of those declining an interview. Two competent interviewers were used throughout and public co-operation was encouraging, so that the refusal rate was kept down to the relatively low figure of 12 per cent. The people who were unwilling to give an interview were for the most part preoccupied with other business or of an apathetic disposition. They do not appear to have included any significant proportion of people with unpopular opinions.

We propose to run through the survey questions one by one, reporting the main results. This procedure will not, unfortunately, do justice to some of the interesting details or the wealth of comment offered by the subjects. Further information may, however, be available on application to the author.

QUESTION I. *Have you any personal connection with any of the British Colonies or Dominions, perhaps through friends or relatives?*

Yes — total 37 per cent. English localities (Ipswich, Alcester, Leeds and Coventry combined) — 27 per cent; Scottish localities (Hawick and Leith) — 55 per cent.

QUESTIONS II AND III. 36 per cent of those interviewed had a rough idea of the difference between colonies and dominions. After all had been reminded that 'Dominions are countries like Australia and Canada which run their own Government; Colonies are to some extent dependent on Britain for their Government': 62 per cent were able to offer the names of two or more supposed colonies, and 43 per cent to name two or more *correctly*. The following were named most frequently:

Jamaica	68 times	New Zealand	28 times
Ceylon	43 ,,	Nigeria	27 ,,
Kenya	40 ,,	Malta	27 ,,
West Indies	35 ,,	India	27 ,,
Cyprus	33 ,,	Canada	22 ,,
Australia	31 ,,	British Guiana	21 ,,
South Africa	29 ,,		

Scots were better informed and more accurate than English people: 53 per cent of Scots respondents gave the names of two or more colonies correctly compared with 38 per cent from England; 85 per cent of the names they offered were correct in contrast to 58 per cent on the part of English respondents.

QUESTION IV. *Are we doing anything in the colonies to teach the people there to govern themselves?*

Yes — 79 per cent; No — 1 per cent; Don't know and other replies — 20 per cent. (Responses to this question are discussed in Chapter V.)

QUESTION V. *Do you think that we could give more help to the colonies than we do? Or do you think we are giving enough or too much?*

More — 33 per cent; Enough — 34 per cent; Too much — 6 per cent; Don't know and other — 27 per cent.

QUESTION VI. *Do you think this country would be better off or worse off without the colonies?*

Better off — 10 per cent; Worse off — 69 per cent; Don't know and other — 21 per cent. Other answers included such views as: 'We would be better off if we treated them in a way that would ensure their backing us up'; 'Colonies haven't helped us much, it's we who've done the helping. But the Dominions are a different kettle of fish. They've helped us financially with their products, like tin, tea, rubber and coffee.'

QUESTION VII. *You probably know that coloured people from the colonies often come here either to study or to find work. Have you yourself ever come across such coloured people? (i) How did you come across them? (ii) What countries did they come from? (iii) Have you ever had a personal friend or someone you knew very well who was coloured?*

45 per cent had 'come across' coloured immigrants — responses varying from 22 and 30 per cent in Alcester and Hawick, to 56 and 60 per cent in Leith and Ipswich. They had been met more frequently at work than elsewhere and were most frequently said to come from India, West Indies, Jamaica and Africa. 11 per cent replied that they had known a coloured person very well, the variation being from 4 per cent in rural Alcester to 20 per cent in Coventry. This may be compared with the fact that coloured people constitute less than half of one per cent of the British population.

QUESTION VIII. *Have you ever had any experiences which have influenced you for or against coloured people?*

9 per cent reported favourable and 1 per cent unfavourable experiences. It is interesting to note that of the fifteen respondents who by a subsequent classification were scaled as 'unfriendly' or 'very unfriendly', not one reported any unfavourable experiences; nearly all replied with a blank 'no'. This question drew a considerable number of sympathetic comments and affirmations of equality.

QUESTION IX. *Provided, of course, there is plenty of work about, do you think that coloured colonials should be allowed to go on coming to this country?*

Unequivocal 'yes' — 37 per cent; affirmative answers qualified by some reference to housing shortage, or by repetition of the proviso in the question — 35 per cent (however, any distinction between these respondents and those of the former category must be very artificial); other replies — 9 per cent; don't know — 1 per cent; outright 'no' — 18 per cent. (See Chapter V.)

QUESTION X. *Coloured people born in our colonies are, of course, British subjects like ourselves. Do you think that they should, therefore, be admitted to this country in preference to European foreigners like Italians and Poles?*

Yes — 71 per cent; No — 13 per cent (some of these were opposed, not to coloured immigration but to any restrictions on a person's freedom to immigrate).

QUESTION XI. *Do you think any one kind of coloured immigrant or people from any particular place make better citizens of this country than others?*

This question was included to see how far respondents were aware of differences between West Indians and Pakistanis or others. 18 per cent replied 'yes', most of them commenting favourably on West Indians' or Jamaicans' ability to settle in. Sikh pedlars (referred to as 'those men with cases') seemed to be disliked in Leith, the most tolerant of the six localities. In a number of cases the conduct of white and coloured American troops was compared, much to the advantage of the latter.

QUESTION XII. *What do you think most people would feel about working with a coloured person?*

QUESTION XIII. *What would you yourself feel about working with a coloured person?*

Would dislike it: self—6 per cent; most people would—19 per cent. Would not mind: self—71 per cent; most people would not—23 per cent. Varied responses: self, would be mildly against it, or it would depend on circumstances—17 per cent; most people, some would be against, depend on circumstances—39 per cent. Don't know and other replies: self—6 per cent, most people 19 per cent. The contrast between subjects' own views and their estimate of others' is remarkable. These questions elicited many comments protesting the subjects' own belief in equality and anger over the suspiciousness or superior attitudes of others.

QUESTION XIV. *Many coloured people have difficulty in finding lodgings or accommodation. Which of these three things do you think we should do to get over these difficulties? (i) Make it easier for them to get rooms in hotels and boarding houses? (ii) Ask more private people to have them stay in their houses? (iii) Provide hostels for them? Why do you think this is best?*

(i) or (ii) favoured by 12 per cent; and in association with hostels, by a further 10 per cent. Hostels were thought by 26 per cent to be suitable for new arrivals, for single people, or as a protection against prejudice; 45 per cent suggested hostels for reasons implying that separation was more appropriate, or for no ascertained reason; 2 per cent answered 'none of these', either because they were opposed to immigration or because they thought special arrangements ill advised; 6 per cent gave no classifiable reply. (Responses to this question are discussed briefly in Chapter V.)

QUESTION XV. *Sometimes landladies and hotels refuse to take in coloured people. Is this right or wrong? If wrong, what if their business may suffer?*

Right — 12 per cent; Wrong — 52 per cent; 'Up to them' — 22 per cent; Other answers — 11 per cent; Don't know — 4 per cent. (See Chapter V.)

QUESTION XVI. *Would you mind having coloured people as neighbours?
Would you say you were one of the people who believe in keeping themselves to themselves?*

10 per cent objected to coloured people as neighbours; 81 per cent
said they would not mind and the remainder gave no clear reply.
Responses were more clear-cut than those to questions XII-XIV,
suggesting that coloured people were more acceptable as neighbours
than in more intimate relationships. Among the comments we note:

'You haven't any choice, though they don't come in council
houses at present.' — Coventry housewife.

'They'd be better than our present neighbours.' — Several
subjects.

'I wouldn't mind. I don't like neighbours much.' — Two subjects.

'No, but not too many. They're just like the Jews — now we get
off the pavements for them. They monopolize Leeds. Perhaps the
coloureds will go the same way.' — Similar observations from
two Leeds workers.

The second part of this question was included purely on speculation.
The phrase 'I keep myself to myself' occurs repeatedly in discussion of
neighbourhood relations and seems to be of considerable significance
to the speakers. Its recall in this interview did not provoke any reactions of interest to the central topic, though we note that the question
appeared meaningful to a high proportion of subjects. Only 3 per cent
failed to answer yes or no. The more industrial a locality the higher the
proportion of affirmative answers. The more rural it was, the more
negatives. Thus Leeds — 76 per cent 'yes', 16 per cent 'no'; Coventry
— 60/40 per cent; Ipswich — 54/42 per cent; Hawick — 52/42 per cent;
Leith — 48 50 per cent; Alcester — 44/50 per cent. The only exception
is Leith which, originally a small seaport, is now part of the city of
Edinburgh.

The last part of the interview was rather different. Three cards had
been prepared, each bearing ten statements about immigration, coloured people and relations between the two groups. The interviewer
handed over these cards one by one saying that these were the sort of

things that had been said about these topics and inviting the subject to indicate which statements, if any, represented the respondent's own views on the matter. He was simply to say those he agreed with; there was to be no forcing a person to express an opinion about a question he had never considered and about which he held no views. Some people responded fairly readily, expressing agreement with half the statements on the card, or more, and sometimes assenting to contradictory propositions. Others considered each one very carefully and assented to one or two only, and, on occasion, to none at all of the ten. In the circumstances, therefore, it was impressive that one statement received the assent of 76 per cent, and two of nearly 70 per cent of the people interviewed.

TABLE V

Responses to Statements on Immigration

Proposition	Percentage Assenting	Contradictory*	Position on Card
1. Coloured people are just as good as us when they have the same training and opportunities	76	6	1–10
2. A lot of the coloured people here are very clever	68	7	2–5
3. If we all behaved in a more Christian way there would not be any colour problem	67	—	3–8
4. It would be a good thing if people of different races mixed with one another more	62	3	1–8
5. People who treat others badly because of their colour ought to be punished	57	14	3–3
6. Coloured peoples from different countries are quite different from each other	52	5	2–2
7. Coloured people are all right if you treat them just like any other white person	51	20	3–2
8. Good-class coloured people are all right	51	15	3–5
9. English (or Scottish) people are too slow in making friends with strangers	47	—	1–3
10. The present immigration of coloured people is a serious problem	47	1	1–1
11. People of all races agree about the most important things in life	46	—	2–3
12. Things will be all right when people get used to coloured people	41	45	1–6
13. Coloured men are welcome to live here if they don't marry English (or Scottish) girls	39	—	1–7
14. You cannot be sure how coloured people are going to behave	38	—	3–9

203

Proposition	Percentage Assenting	Contradictory*	Position on Card
15. The Africans and West Indians have their own religions at home	36	13	2–7
16. Coloured people are all right but they need to be handled differently from white people	33	20	3–1
17. Coloured people have stronger sexual urges than white people	30	1	2–9
18. The present immigration of coloured people is not a serious problem	29	1	1–2
19. The Africans and West Indians are nearly all Christians	24	13	2–8
20. The trouble is that most of the coloured people in Britain are of poor class	22	15	3–6
21. It is no use trying to punish people who treat others badly because of their colour. This is best left to public opinion	21	14	3–4
22. The coloured people have their own friends and do not want us to bother them	20	—	3–7
23. If you try to make friends with a coloured person he will think you are doing it just because he is coloured and may not like it	17	—	3–10
24. All the coloured people in Britain are pretty much the same	16	5	2–1
25. People of a different race can never learn our way of life	15	5	1–5
26. Coloured people will always be inferior to white people	10	6	1–9
27. All mixing between races should be avoided	9	3	1–4
28. Most of the coloured people here are very ignorant	9	7	2–6
29. Coloured people do not have stronger sexual urges than white people	9	1	2–10
30. The coloured people who come here are uncivilized	4	—	2–4

* Where two statements were contradictory or of opposite implication the number of subjects assenting to both is given. Some of those scored are not strictly incompatible (e.g. Nos. 2 and 28; 8 and 20). Scottish people much less frequently assented to contrary propositions; however, the response rate was generally lower in Scotland.

Responses to the different propositions are set out in Table V, but in view of the frequency with which subjects misunderstood some of them these figures are to be interpreted with caution. The interviewers were instructed to note as carefully as possible all the comments subjects made while examining the cards, and it is clear from certain entries that the formal responses failed to represent or even negated the subject's true views. Any attempt to score answers according to the subject's true opinions instead of formal acceptance of statements would, however, be most hazardous in view of the fact that the more taciturn subjects offered few comments by which to make such a check. We propose instead to indicate where formal response rates seem unreliable in the light of this additional material.

It is open to question whether this method of opinion-surveying is suitable for use with so heterogeneous a sample as that obtained from the electoral rolls. For some subjects the statements were not simple enough; others complained, not unreasonably, of their naivety. However, other methods might have invested responses with a rigidity and consistency unrepresentative of people's true states of mind. The great majority of respondents understood the propositions full well, and despite the occasional weakness of our techniques the general import of what they have to say is unmistakable.

Careful study of each subject's answers to all the questions shows that the general tendency is in fact far more favourable towards coloured people than the figures by themselves imply, and that the response to unfavourable statements is partly accounted for by the tendency of subjects friendly to coloured people — even extremely friendly — to assent to two or three unfavourable propositions. Often this was due to misunderstanding. In view of the position elsewhere it is notable that at no stage did any one of the three hundred people interviewed argue that coloured people were biologically inferior or that there were any biological differences relevant to questions of social equality. Coloured people might at present be at a disadvantage, but this was because they had not had the same opportunities, while in any case their turn to be leaders might be on the way. Though they discounted biological differences the people interviewed showed themselves appreciative of cultural variations. Many felt that the pattern of racial relations in the colonies was no guide to relations in Britain.

The response to Proposition No. 1 is quite unambiguous, but that to its antithesis, No. 26, calls for some comment. No one explicitly concurred with the key word 'always'. The most positive assent was 'Whites and blacks started off at the same time and we have advanced and they haven't. Therefore they are inferior'; and this came from a man who expressed many sentiments favourable to the immigrants.

Other comments from people assenting cast doubt on their assent, e.g. 'Perhaps this is because you can't understand them'; 'They are at present in the sense that any repressed people are inferior, but they certainly won't always be'; 'Inferior to some whites because they won't let themselves go'. Close examination suggests that the view expressed in this statement cannot have been truly accepted by any more than 2 per cent of the sample. The same is true of Proposition No. 28, paired with No. 2. The high response to No. 3 is indicative of the general view that racial relations pose a moral problem independent of any biological questions. The comments of those dissenting from this statement rarely counter this conclusion: e.g. 'The colour problem is the fact of bringing them into this country'; 'Christian way? It was Christians who crucified Christ!' Some people opposed to social segregation would not assent to the fourth statement because they took it to refer to intermarriage.

Proposition No. 5 was probably the most misunderstood, e.g. 'Don't be unkind'; 'They are human; treat them fair'; 'Bias against them is all wrong'. But despite this, and the high rate of contradiction, the much stronger response to No. 5 than to No. 21 does reflect a widely held view put into words by a Coventry housewife: 'Leave it to the law, for public opinion wouldn't punish them — they'd say it's only a black man.' Nos. 6 and 24 showed up our respondents' awareness of differences in their own community; a Scot pointed out 'We're different from the English'; while an Ipswich woman observed 'They seem alike because I don't know any well, but they can't *be* all the same.' Propositions Nos. 7 and 16 were also frequently misinterpreted, as the level of contradiction would suggest. Relatively few savoured the wording of No. 16 ('Handled? I don't like that word'); many interpreted it favourably, e.g. 'In a sense, because they are more sensitive about some things on account of the arrogant way British people behave in the colonies'; those who responded to both seemed more inclined to No. 7, e.g. 'There's nothing like kindness'; 'Being called "niggers" they do object to'; 'They ought to be treated like anyone else too, provided they're not the up-to-London-for-the-women type.' Another high level of contradiction is found with the statements relating to class. The general feeling (as experienced by a Leeds worker assenting to No. 8) was 'All people are all right if you treat them right – you can't just class people.' Many respondents rejected the underlying idea by implication, and some quite explicitly: 'Class rather gets me down'; 'I don't believe in class'; 'This is a silly question.'

Assent to Proposition No. 9 was much heavier in the urban areas: Coventry 68 per cent, Ipswich 66 per cent, Leith 62 per cent, Leeds 48 per cent, Hawick 36 per cent and Alcester 16 per cent. Proposition No. 11 was not particularly successful owing to uncertainty as to its interpretation; respondents showed considerable awareness of cultural and individual diversity, often expressing scepticism of any rigid categories in this respect. Nos. 12 and 25 may also be paired. Some of those responding to No. 25 did so on account of misunderstanding ('In wartime there was no question about colour bar, so why worry now?') While people who did not agree to No. 12 were often in fundamental agreement with it (e.g. 'We *are* used to coloured people' – from Ipswich). Some were genuinely doubtful ('Some of their ways we could never get used to – they don't learn how to queue up and so on'), but the balance is overwhelming for No. 12.

Responses to the statement disapproving of intermarriage are of particular interest. The true rate of assent definitely lies over 45 per cent, though nearly one person in four went out of his way to dissent and say he (or she) did not disapprove of it. Most of the dissenters thought this a question for the individuals concerned ('How can anyone stop them if they love each other?'), or approved of it as a path to peace ('If there's one way of breaking down colour bar it's through marriage'). Those who argued against intermarriage confined themselves to stating what they felt – 'it's not right', 'looks peculiar', 'not natural', etc. – or objected on account of the children: 'Everything about the colour bar comes back to this – the children suffer'; 'It's hard luck on the children being half-castes.' This distinction between marriage and parenthood seems to be a very real one and of particular interest because it is not found in the better-known situations of racial contact. One of our subjects met the interviewer a day or two later and stopped her to say that he had been thinking hard about the question and had come to the conclusion that he had no objection at all to mixed couples getting married provided they didn't have children. Similar views were expressed in the interviews.

Proposition No. 14, though it accords with our argument in the text, was not well received. Some people concurred ('You never know how to take them sort'; 'The coloured woman at our works never speaks and we don't know what she thinks. Some say she's kind, but I don't know'), yet over a third of those assenting added that the same could be said of white people. Propositions Nos. 15 and 19 have been referred to in Chapter II, and so have Nos. 17 and 29. Belief that coloured people have stronger sexual urges was usually based on hearsay or ideas as to the effects of climate ('Where there's sun there's a difference'), though there was some scepticism (occasionally of a self-defeating kind as with the Coventry man who complained 'I only know from books and you can't believe all you read'). Among the comments of those assenting to No. 17 there are some which weaken the reliability of the response rate, e.g. 'Foreigners are hot-blooded', and 'But the girls lead them on', while some of those dissenting argue 'All they do we do — but we do it under cover, which is worse'. If our theories are correct the low response to propositions Nos. 22 and 23 (as well as No. 14) would suggest that the general public are not conscious of the factors making relations with coloured people uncertain. There was some agreement with No. 23: 'They think you are making fun of them'; 'A business friendship he wouldn't mind but the "good deed" type they don't like.' But many said either that this was contrary to their experience or suspected it as a rationalization: 'Don't agree: it's an excuse used by white people'; 'They aren't that dumb. They know when you're being proper friendly. At work we use strong gloves. I lend them mine and vice versa, never thinking whether a black or a white hand goes into them.' This last comment, however, raises the query whether those who deny Proposition No. 23 are not drawing upon experience at work where the nature of the relationship is clearly defined and suspicions about 'good deeds' do not arise.

Opposition to the last statement was stronger than the low response of 4 per cent would suggest. Probably half of those accepting it did not really believe this, to judge by their comments, like: 'Some of them', and 'The veneer of civilization is thinner — but they're not uncivilized.' The comments of others emphasized that they did not feel entitled to pass judgment upon other peoples: 'As much — say, as much as us'; 'Lots of Irish — like myself — are uncivilized'; 'Some of them, but then the biggest half of us are uncivilized too.'

It was not intended at the outset to score individual subject's responses and rate them on a scale of friendliness–unfriendliness, and the items used had not been pre-tested for this purpose. Nevertheless it was decided after a preliminary inspection of the material obtained that this might be worth attempting retrospectively. A scale was evolved by an

TABLE VI

Correlations between Sex of Respondents and Friendliness towards Immigrants

	% Males	% Females	$D/\sigma_D{_\rho}$	Result
Very friendly	19	23	0·85	Females predominate
Friendly	39	38	0·18	Not significant
Indeterminate	8	6	0·67	Males predominate
Contradictory	17	15	0·48	Males predominate
Unfriendly (all)	8	3	1·92	Males predominate

adaptation of the Thurstone technique: 43 statements taken from the interview schedule were submitted to a panel of 50 judges, formed from members of the university staff and their wives. The judges were asked to arrange such statements as they could in eleven categories. Those about which there was serious disagreement were discarded, leaving 22 statements as basis for rating. Subjects were finally categorized: very friendly; friendly; indeterminate; contradictory; unfriendly; very unfriendly and unresponsive.

Tables to show correlations between friendliness–unfriendliness and sex, age and income groups were constructed. These were tested for significance taking a value of $D/\sigma_D{_\rho} = 3$ as the lowest acceptable. That is to say, we rejected all variations unless the possibility of their occurring by chance was less than one in a thousand. Table VI shows that male respondents were significantly more unfriendly and females more friendly. No pattern of correlation was found with either age or income group.

In districts where people were relatively well acquainted with coloured immigrants (Coventry, Ipswich, Leeds, Leith) responses were sometimes more favourable than in the relatively out of the way localities (Alcester, Hawick). No association was found, however, between subjects' friendliness and the experience of contact or friendship with coloured people reported under Proposition No. 7.

The results of this survey demonstrate that — however the term be defined — colour prejudice is not widespread in Great Britain. But the evidence of discrimination is undeniable. Unless the situation changes, any future inquiry that rejects our conclusions will therefore have to furnish a better explanation of the paradox which was our starting-point — why should coloured people so often be shabbily treated when the vast majority of individual Britons are favourably disposed towards them?

NOTES, REFERENCES
AND BIBLIOGRAPHY

NOTES AND REFERENCES

PREFACE
[1] The incident recalled in the third paradox is taken from Mary Trevelyan, *From the Ends of the Earth*, London 1942, p. 53.

CHAPTER I: PREJUDICE AND DISCRIMINATION
[1] Carey McWilliams, *Brothers Under the Skin*, Boston 1951, p. 315.

[2] The impossibility of defining discrimination both in objective terms and as something morally wrong is shown in *The Coloured Quarter*, pp. 120-1.

[3] S. F. Nadel's discussion of the concepts 'individual' and 'person' is to be found in his *The Foundations of Social Anthropology*, London 1951, pp. 91-5.

[4] For the distinction between intention and motive see John Macmurray, *The Boundaries of Science*, London 1939, pp. 239-49 and 255; also p. 92.

CHAPTER II: EXPLAINING PREJUDICE
[1] O. Mannoni, *Prospero and Caliban*, London 1956, p. 200.

[2] John Dollard, 'Hostility and Fear in Social Life', *Social Forces*, vol. 17, 1938, pp. 15-26.

[3] E. L. Hartley, *Problems in Prejudice*, New York 1946.

[4] T. W. Adorno *et al.*, *The Authoritarian Personality*, New York 1950.

[5] H. J. Eysenck, *The Structure of Human Personality*, London 1953, ch. VIII.

[6] For criticism of Eysenck's work see *Psychological Bulletin*, vol. 53, 1956.

[7] James H. Robb, *Working-Class Anti-Semite*, London 1955.

[8] Attention should be drawn to the dependence of Mr Richmond's theory upon the assumption of widespread insecurity amongst the British population. Thus in *The Colour Problem*, p. 240, he states that 'there is now conclusive evidence to suggest that ... roughly one third [of the population] is extremely prejudiced'. Severe prejudice having been described as 'a response to inner feelings of anxiety and insecurity which have their origins deep in the unconscious mind, and are often derived from early childhood experiences of deprivation or frustration'. It may be objected that there is no satisfactory (let alone 'conclusive') evidence of the proportion of the population who are prejudiced as Mr Richmond uses the term; nor is there evidence of insecurity and childhood deprivation on the scale conceived.

[9] Mr Richmond has recently reformulated his propositions to give more weight to institutional factors: 'Recent Researches on Race Relations in Britain', *Int. Soc. Sci. Bull.*, vol. X, 1958, pp. 344-72.

[10] On the two uses of the word 'stereotype' see D. Krech and R. S. Crutchfield, *Theory and Problems of Social Psychology*, New York 1948, pp. 171-2.

[11] H. J. Eysenck, 'War and Aggressiveness: A Survey of Social Attitude Studies.' Ch. III of T. H. Pear (ed.), *Psychological Factors in Peace and War*, London 1950.

[12] *The Authoritarian Personality*, p. 56.

CHAPTER III: EXPLAINING DISCRIMINATION
[1] T. H. Marshall, *Citizenship and Social Class*, Cambridge 1950, p. 103.

[2] On social factors affecting the perception of colour, see H. E. O. James and Cora Tenen, 'How Adolescents think of People', *British Journal of Psychology*, vol. XLI, 1950, esp. pp. 169-72; also Gunnar Myrdal *et al.*, *An American Dilemma*, New York 1944, pp. 683-4.

[3] Oliver Cromwell Cox, *Caste, Class and Race*, New York 1948, p. 393.

[4] Carey McWilliams, *op. cit.*, pp. 345-6.

[5] This passage is quoted with Dr Landes's kind permission.

[6] *Negroes in Britain*, p. 232.

[7] 'Race and Society', reprinted in the UNESCO volume *The Race Question in Modern Science*, London 1957, pp. 203-4.

[8] *Colonial Students*, p. 68-71 and 154-6.

[9] The functionalist school in sociology adopted a position similar to the Marxist in holding that 'sentiments ... are developed in the individual by the action of society upon him' – A. R. Radcliffe-Brown, *The Andaman Islanders*, London 1953, p. 234.

[10] Meyer Fortes, 'Social Anthropology', in *Scientific Thought in the Twentieth Century*, ed. A. E. Heath, London 1951, p. 332.

[11] My argument here is directed against F. A. Hayek's view that the data of the social sciences are the acts and opinions of individuals and are hence 'subjective' as opposed to the 'objective' data of the natural sciences; cf. *The Counter-Revolution of Science*, Glencoe 1952, p. 28 *et passim*.

CHAPTER IV: CHANGING CONCEPTIONS OF THE COLOURED MAN

[1] Philip Thicknesse, quoted by Cedric Dover, *Hell in the Sunshine*, London 1943, p. 159. Thicknesse had formerly been an army officer in Jamaica. The first known record of governmental concern about colonial immigration dates from 11th August, 1596, when, according to the *Acts of the Privy Council* 'Her Majestie understanding that there are of late divers blackmoores brought into this realme, of which kinde of people there are allready too manie, consideringe howe God hath blessed this land with great increase of people of our owne nation ... those kinde of people should be sent forth of the lande ... '

[2] The judicial decisions regarding slavery in England are discussed in Edward Fiddes, 'Lord Mansfield and the Somersett Case', *Law Quarterly Review*, vol. 50, 1934, pp. 499-511.

[3] On the 'noble savage' see Yrjö Hirn, *Goda Vildar och Ädla Rovare*, Stockholm 1941, pp. 11-12 and 209 *ad fin.*, esp. 256-7. On the anti-slavery literature of the eighteenth century, see Wylie Sypher, *Guinea's Captive Kings*, Chapel Hill 1942.

[4] Regarding Negro servants, cf. 'The practice of importing Negroe servants into these kingdoms is said to be already a grievance that requires a remedy, and yet it is every day encouraged, insomuch that the number in this metropolis only, is supposed to be near 20,000; the main objection to their importation is, that they cease to consider themselves as slaves in this free country, nor will they put up with an inequality of treatment, nor more willingly perform the laborious offices of servitude than our own people, and if put to do it, are generally fullen spiteful, treacherous and revengeful. It is therefore highly impolitic to introduce them as servants here where that rigour and severity is impracticable which is absolutely necessary to make them useful' – *Gentleman's Magazine*, vol. xxxiv, 1764, p. 492. There are also references in *Negroes in Britain* and *The Coloured Quarter*. A remarkable miscellany of historical information is assembled in J. A. Rogers, *Sex and Race: Negro-Caucasian Mixing in All Ages and All Lands*, 3 vols., New York 1940; and the same author's *Nature Knows No Colour Line*.

[5] The Cambridge sermon is quoted from G. R. Mellor, *British Imperial Trusteeship, 1783-1950*, London 1951, p. 44.

[6] R. F. Burton, in *Mem. Anth. Soc. London*, vol. I, 1863-4, p. 321.

[7] Alfred C. Haddon, *History of Anthropology*, London 1934; and Sir Arthur Keith in *J. Roy. Anth. Inst.*, vol. XLVII, 1917, for the split between the two societies.

[8] Frank H. Hankins, *The Racial Basis of Civilization*, New York 1931.

[9] F. E. Faverty, *Matthew Arnold the Ethnologist*, Illinois 1951.

[10] Galton, like many of his contemporaries, thought a scientific morality possible. The Eugenics Society still pursues this chimera – to judge by its recent pamphlet *West Indian Immigration*. It is now more widely appreciated that whereas scientific research can provide information useful to us in deciding upon questions of value, it cannot itself pronounce upon values.

[11] J. R. Seeley, *The Expansion of England*, London 1883, pp. 357-8.

[12] J. A. Cramb, *The Origins and Destiny of Imperial Britain*, London 1900 and 1915.

[13] William L. Langer, *The Diplomacy of Imperialism*, New York 1951, Ch. 3.

[14] Article 'Telegony', *Encyclopaedia Britannica*, 11th edn., 1911.

CHAPTER V: THE ARCHETYPAL STRANGER

[1] George Santayana, *Soliloquies in England*, London 1922, p. 32.

[2] George C. Homans, in *The Listener*, 16th August, 1956, p. 232.

[3] George Orwell, *England, Your England*, 1953, p. 28.

[4] The Oxbridge girl student's remarks are quoted from Sheila Webster's MS.

[5] Margaret Mead and Rhoda Metraux (eds.), *The Study of Culture at a Distance*, Chicago 1953, pp. 19 and 404.

[6] On 'the fear of strangers', Geoffrey Gorer in *Horizon*, vol. xx, 1949, p. 376. Cf. Michael Banton, *West African City*, London 1957, pp. 109-17.

[7] Gustav Jahoda argues very plausibly that a migrant can never internalize the norms of a new culture as he did those of the culture in which he grew up: 'The Overlap of Value Systems' (*unpublished lecture*).

[8] Elizabeth Bott, *Family and Social Network*, London 1957, Ch. VI.

[9] Cf. *Neighbourhood and Community*, Liverpool University Department of Social Science, 1954.

[10] H. J. Eysenck, *The Psychology of Politics*, London 1954, pp. 84-7.

CHAPTER VI: WHEN CUSTOM FAILS

[1] Carl Linnaeus, *Systema Naturae*, 12th edn., 1760. This, an extreme expression of the Enlightenment, may be contrasted with the opposite view as expressed by G. K. Chesterton: 'We are never free until some institution frees us, and liberty cannot exist until it is declared by authority'. *Manalive*, London 1912. Penguin edition, p. 36.

[2] Lord Altrincham recently resigned from two committees of the Victoria League owing to his opposition to their policy of not admitting coloured students to mixed hostels.

[3] Max Gluckman, *The Judicial Process among the Barotse*, Manchester 1955, p. 19.

[4] Carey, *Colonial Students*, pp. 62-3.

[5] P.E.P., *Colonial Students in Britain*, p. 224.

[6] *The Coloured Quarter*, p. 148.

[7] Carey, *op. cit.*, pp. 60-1.

[8] Michael Young and Peter Willmott, *Family and Kinship in East London*, London 1957, p. 129.

[9] Clarence Senior and Douglas Manley, *A Report on Jamaican Migration to Great Britain*, Kingston 1955, p. 45.

[10] P.E.P., *op. cit.*, p. 224.

[11] The actor does not select the norms he considers relevant to the situation. Were this so we would have to seek the criteria he employs in selecting them, and then the criteria for those criteria, and so on back in an infinite regression. The norms are fixed. The actor has to decide if a particular situation falls within the orbit of one rather than another, and if he decides wrongly he may be penalized.

[12] James and Tenen, *op. cit.*, p. 170.

[13] H. D. Willcock, 'The effect of interviewers' own opinions about minorities and foreigners on the opinions about coloured people which they obtained or recorded from informants.' Stencil.

CHAPTER VII: STRANGERS IN DOCKLAND

[1] F. A. Richardson, *Social Conditions in Ports and Dockland Areas*, London 1935, pp. 4-5.

[2] James Weldon Johnson, *Along This Way*, 1933, Penguin edition 1941, p. 163.

[3] George Lamming, *The Emigrants*, London 1954, and Samuel Selvon, *The Lonely Londoners*, London 1956.

[4] The views of intermarriage are quoted from the Press Summary, *Coloured People in Great Britain*.

CHAPTER VIII: RACE AND CLASS AT THE UNIVERSITIES

[1] P.E.P., *op. cit.*, p. 73.

[2] Jean-Paul Sartre, *Portrait of the Anti-Semite*, London 1948.

[3] 'Black Orpheus', English translation in *Présence Africaine*, nos. 10-11.

CHAPTER IX: COLOURED WORKERS IN INDUSTRIAL CITIES

[1] *Birmingham Post*, 25th September, 1954.

[2] For figures of immigration see Caribbean Welfare Service Reports.

[3] Quoted from *Reynolds News*, 9th September, 1956, by kind permission of the Editor.

[4] The proportion of West Indians drawing National Assistance is very small. Cf. Senior's *Report*, p. 40. In December 1958 about 14,000 coloured immigrants were drawing unemployment benefit or national assistance.

[5] *Manchester Guardian*, 22nd February, 1955.

[6] J. F. Skone and S. Clayton, 'An Inquiry into the Housing, Health, and Welfare of Immigrant Coloured Persons in a Midland County Borough', *The Medical Officer*, 1st March, 1957, pp. 121-6.

CHAPTER X: QUOD ERAT DEMONSTRANDUM

[1] For interesting comments on the contemporary significance of racial sentiments, see W. R. Crocker, *The Racial Factor in International Relations*, Canberra 1956.

[2] Maurice Freedman (ed.), *A Minority in Britain*, London 1955, pp. 223-6; on Negroes in the northern states of the U.S., cf. Myrdal, *op. cit.*, pp. 599-604. The parallels between the position of Negroes in Britain and in Brazil are also much closer than is commonly believed. After the public outcry following the barring of Miss Katherine Dunham from a São Paulo hotel, the government in 1951 enacted legislation against racial discrimination; imprisonment for up to twelve months can be imposed for serious infringements.

[3] For further argument to the effect that sociological generalizations are not confined to historical periods, see Karl R. Popper, *The Poverty of Historicism*, London 1957, pp. 97-104.

APPENDIX I: TEN COMMANDMENTS OF INTER-GROUP RELATIONS

[1] Percy Bysshe Shelley, *In Defence of Poetry*.

[2] These propositions are in part reprinted and in part paraphrased from *A Manual of Intergroup Relations*, by John P. Dean and Alex Rosen, by permission of the University of Chicago Press. Copyright 1955 by the University of Chicago.

[3] On legislation against racial discrimination, see *The Coloured Quarter*, pp. 238-45, and references there cited.

BIBLIOGRAPHY

General

BANTON, MICHAEL. *The Coloured Quarter*, London (Jonathan Cape), 1955. West African and West Indian immigrants in the East End of London.

CAREY, A. T. *Colonial Students*, London (Secker & Warburg), 1956. A study of the social adaptation of coloured students in London.

COLLINS, SYDNEY. *Coloured Minorities in Britain*, London (Lutterworth), 1957. Describes Afro–West Indian, Arab, Chinese and other settlements in port areas.

EGGINGTON, JOYCE. *They Seek a Living* (Hutchinson), 1957. A journalist's account of the West Indian migration 1948-56.

INSTITUTE OF RACE RELATIONS. *Coloured People in Great Britain*, a monthly summary of news and comments in the Press. March 1955 to date.

JAMES, H. E. O. AND TENEN, CORA. *The Teacher was Black*, London (Heinemann), 1953. Schoolchildren's reactions to two African teachers.

LITTLE, K. L. *Negroes in Britain*, London (Routledge & Kegan Paul), 1948. Cardiff dockland and its coloured population; the history of Negroes in this country and the development of racial attitudes.

P.E.P. (POLITICAL AND ECONOMIC PLANNING). *Colonial Students in Britain*. London (P.E.P.), 1955. Colonial students and arrangements made for them.

RICHMOND, ANTHONY H. *Colour Prejudice in Britain*, London (Routledge & Kegan Paul), 1954. A study of West Indian workers in Liverpool, 1941-51, and their social adjustment.

SENIOR, CLARENCE AND MANLEY, DOUGLAS. *A Report on Jamaican Migration to Great Britain*, Kingston (Jamaican Government publication), 1955. Migrants' difficulties and progress.

Unpublished Works

DRAKE, ST CLAIR. *Value Systems, Social Structure, and Race Relations in the British Isles*, Ph.D. thesis, University of Chicago, 1954. Microfilmed.

GARIGUE, PHILIP. *Colonial Students in London*, MS., 1952.

JUNOD, VIOLAINE IDELETTE. *Report on a study of the Coloured 'Social Elite' in London*, MS., 1952.

LANDES, RUTH. *Colour in Britain*, MS., 1953.

NDEM, EYO BASSEY. *Negro Immigrants in Manchester*, MS., 1953.

PATTERSON, SHEILA. MSS *re* West Indian Settlement in South London.

WEBSTER, SHEILA. *Negroes in Bluebrick*. Unpublished MS. Department of Social Anthropology, University of Edinburgh.

Articles and Pamphlets

DRAKE, ST CLAIR. 'The "Colour Problem" in Britain: A Study in Social Definitions', *Sociological Review*, N.S., vol. 3, 1956, pp. 197-217.

MANLEY, DOUGLAS. 'The Formal Associations of a Negro Community in Britain', *Social and Economic Studies*, vol. 4, 1955, pp. 231-44.

BIBLIOGRAPHY

MAUNDER, W. F. 'The New Jamaican Emigration', *Social and Economic Studies*, vol. 4, 1955, pp. 38–63.

NDEM, EYO B. 'The Status of Coloured People in Britain', *Phylon*, vol. XVIII, 1957, pp. 82–7.

REID, JANET. 'Negro Workers in Manchester', *Sociological Review*, N.S., vol. 4, 1956, pp. 199–211.

STEPHENS, LESLIE. *Employment of Coloured Workers in the Birmingham Area*, London (Institute of Personnel Management), 1956.

INDEX

INDEX

ABRAHAMS, PETER, 160-2
'actor', defined, 19
Adorno, T. W., *et al.*, 213
aggression, direct and displaced, 23
Altrincham, Lord, 215
American Indians, 141, 143
—— South, 18, 23, 25, 41, 92
Ammon, O., 62
anthropology, nineteenth-century, 59-60
antipathy, distinguished from prejudice, 30-1
Anti-semitism, 25, 27, 29, 30, 31, 41, 154, 182
Arnold, Matthew, 63
attitudes, racial, 84-7, 111, 197-210
—— and behaviour, 26-7, 32-3, 37, 48-9, 85, 104, 112-13, 181
Authoritarian Personality, the, 27, 38

BAGEHOT, WALTER, 61
Baker, Sir Samuel, 59
'Big uncles', 159
Birmingham, 160-2
Blumenbach, J. F., 133
Bogardus Social Distance Test, 26, 87-8
Bott, Elizabeth, 215
Brazil, 24, 92, 216
British Council, 93, 148
—— Institute of Public Opinion, 104, 160
Buffon, G., 40
Burton, Sir Richard, 57, 214

CARDIFF, 46, 69, 119, 120
Carey, A. T., 47-9, 93, 101, 149, 213, 215
Carlyle, T., 58
Churches, attitudes of, 59, 121-2, 135
Collins, Sydney, 111
colour, class connotations of, 46-8, 101-2
'colour tax', 47, 49
Columbus, 55
Comte, A., 21
Cox, Oliver Cromwell, 40, 44, 213
Cramb, John Adam, 67-8, 214
Crocker, W. R., 216
cross-breeding, 70
Cypriot immigrants, 84

DARWIN, CHARLES, 60, 64, 70
Dean, John P. and Rosen, A., 187, 216
discrimination, racial, 9, 16, 21, 33, 40-1, 110, 147, 160, 161, 166, 210
—— —— defined, 16-17
—— —— legislation against, 193-4, 216
Dollard, John, 23, 25, 41, 132, 213
Dover, Cedric, 214

EMPLOYMENT, COMPETITION IN, 32, 69, 132, 163, 165, 167
eugenics, 65, 66, 214
Eysenck, H. J., 28, 36, 88, 213, 215

FASCISM, 27, 172
Faverty, F. E., 214
Fiddes, E., 214
Fortes, Meyer, 50, 214
Freedman, M., 216
Freud, S., 24, 25, 48

GALTON, SIR FRANCIS, 64, 65, 66, 214
Glasgow, 162
Gluckman, Max, 97, 215
Gobineau, Count A. de, 62
Gorer, Geoffrey, 82, 83, 215
Grant, Maddison, 63
Gumplowicz, L., 62

HADDON, A. C., 214
Hartley, E. L., 26, 213
Hankins, F. H., 214
Hawaii, 92
Hayek, F. A., 214
Heath, A. E., 214
Heber, Bishop, 57
Hirn, Y., 214
Hogben, Lancelot, 66
Homans, George C., 74, 214
housing conditions, 86, 87, 97, 106, 124, 169
—— societies, 170

IMMIGRANTS, ATTITUDES TO, IN U.S.A., 26
—— numbers of, in Britain, 157-9
—— public health among, 169-70

221

'individual', defined, 19
intermarriage, 100, 129, 134-7, 141, 207
Irish immigrants, 33, 86

JAHODA, GUSTAV, 215
James, H. E. O. and Tenen, C., 112, 213, 215
Johnson, James Weldon, 129, 130, 215
Johnson, Samuel, 56
Junod, Violaine, 150, 151, 152

KEITH, SIR ARTHUR, 214
Kidd, Benjamin, 62, 64
Kipling, R., 68
Krech, D. and Crutchfield, R. S., 213
Kropotkin, Prince Peter, 64
Ku-Klux-Klan, British Branch, 167, 173

LAMMING, GEORGE, 215
Landes, Ruth, 45, 74, 83, 84, 124
Langer, William L., 68, 214
Lapouge, G. B. de, 62
League of Empire Loyalists, 173
Lenin, N., 40
Lightfoot, Bishop, 59
Linnaeus, C., 92, 215
Little, Kenneth, 46, 47, 101, 213
Liverpool, 69, 119
London, Jack, 64

MACMURRAY, JOHN, 213
McWilliams, Carey, 42, 213
Madariaga, Salvador de, 76
Maillaud, Pierre, 74
Maltese immigrants, 84
Manchester, 105, 117, 119, 121
Mannoni, O., 23, 213
Mansfield, Lord, 55
marriage, 100, 129, 131, 133, 141
Marshall, T. H., 39, 213
Marx, Karl, 42
marxist theory of discrimination, 40-4, 49
Mead, Margaret, 77, 215
Mellor, R. G., 214
Mendel, G., 65
Montesquieu, 22
Murphy, Gardner, 25
Myrdal, Gunnar, 213, 216

NADEL, S. F., 20, 213
Ndem, E. B., 105, 117, 121, 124, 125, 127, 128, 129, 130, 131

Nightingale, Florence, 145
'noble savage', 56
'non-person', 130, 179
Notting Hill disturbances, 111, 171

ORWELL, GEORGE, 75, 80, 81, 130, 214
Oxbridge, 70, 75, 108, 138, 140-6

PAKISTANI AND INDIAN IMMIGRANTS, 119, 157-9, 166, 169, 170
—— —— compared with West Indians, 122-4, 182-3
paradoxes, of race relations in Britain, 9, 99, 106, 112, 181, 189, 210
Patterson, Mrs Sheila, 162
Pear, T. H., 213
Pearson, Charles H., 63
Pearson, Karl, 64, 65, 68
P.E.P., 147, 148, 150, 215
'person', social, 20-1, 50, 92-3, 97, 177, 182
Popper, K. R., 216
prejudice, class, 80-1
—— colour, 9, 16, 17, 23ff, 45, 48-9, 75-6, 110, 113, 147, 148, 210
—— defined, 31
professional men, coloured, 105, 150, 181

RACE, USE OF TERM, 10, 39, 42, 63
—— perception of, 40, 64, 139, 140
Radcliffe-Brown, A. R., 22, 214
Reid, Janet, 168
Renier, G. J., 76
Richardson, F. A., 117, 215
Richmond, Anthony H., 32, 33, 34, 35, 49, 213
Robb, James H., 29, 30, 31, 83, 213
Rogers, J. A., 214
Ross, Alan S. C., 80

SANTAYANA, G., 73, 215
Sartre, Jean-Paul, 154, 156, 216
segregation, in colonies, 69, 78
Seeley, Sir J. R., 66, 68, 214
Selvon, Samuel, 215
Senior C. and Manley, D., 104, 215, 216
sex relations, 28, 34, 36-7, 48-9, 70, 83, 128, 130, 132, 141, 179
Shakespeare, W., 133
Shelley, Percy Bysshe, 187, 216
Skone, J. F. and Clayton, S., 216
slaves, Negro, in Britain, 55
slave trade, African, 56-7

social Darwinists, 61, 64, 66
social sanctions, 20, 73, 99, 102, 113, 171
—— sciences, orientations of, 15, 19, 21
sociology of race relations, 10, 15ff, 39ff,
    44ff, 104-5, 179-80
South Shields, 119
Spencer, Herbert, 21, 61, 64, 67
sponsorship, 111
Stepney, 109, 119, 124, 125, 129
stereotypes, 33-7
Stoddard, Lothrop, 64
Sypher, Wylie, 214

'TEDDY BOYS', 38, 171
Tennyson, Lord, 61
Thicknesse, Philip, 55, 214
Thurstone, L., 209
trade unions, 165, 167, 192-3
transport workers, coloured, 163-4
Trevelyan, Mary, 213

'UNCLE TOMS', 155
unemployment, 32, 69, 132, 163, 165, 167
Union Movement, 173

VEBLEN, THORSTEIN, 82

WEBSTER, SHEILA, 70, 75, 87, 88, 108, 138,
    139, 144
Weismann, A., 63
West Indian immigration, 157-9
—— —— immigrants compared with
    Pakistanis and Indians, 122-4, 182-3
Wickenden, James, 171
Willcock, H. D., 215

YOUNG, M. AND WILLMOTT, P., 215